ADVANCE PRAISE

"We have forgotten how to love each other and how to help those we can. The teachings in this book have already saved a dozen lives. The ripple of those lives saved spreads out into hundreds of lives that would have been affected by the loss of any one of those people."

—SHERIDAN'S WIFE

"Sheridan is one of the most amazing humans I have ever had the privilege of knowing. He adopted so many of us who were lost, hurting, or struggling to find our place. His genuine love and dedication to seeing and hearing the broken pieces of lost souls and holding space for the grieving is like nothing I've ever seen before. I am honoured and forever grateful to have him in my life and cannot wait to read what is sure to be a life-changing and life-saving book. Sheridan, you are one of the handful of men in my life that I trust with my heart and I am so damn proud of you."

—SHERIDAN'S SELF-DECLARED PLATONIC SISTER-WIFE

"I've read the rough draft of this book. Almost everyone knows somebody who will benefit from something in Sheridan's words. It will make you cry, it will make you laugh, it will make you feel."

—SHERIDAN'S ACTUAL WIFE'S MOM

"Dad's pretty awesome. 'Speshully now he duzn't yell anymore."

—SHERIDAN'S DOG

"Who is Sheridan? A childhood and lifelong friend of infinite complexity and complex simplicity. A man who has danced on the edge of madness, tangled with his demons, and clawed his way back with all the scars to prove it. A passion for knowledge and understanding. A passion for family. A man who has struggled with and without help. A guy who has found a path back and is empathetic enough to want to share that help with others who are where he has been. A man who fights for balance every day. My brother."

—SHERIDAN'S CLOSEST FRIEND

NOT OKAY? OKAY.

SHERIDAN TAYLOR

NOT OKAY?

OKAY.

A ROADMAP BACK
from the BRINK

HOUNDSTOOTH
PRESS

NOT OKAY? OKAY.
A Roadmap Back from the Brink

FIRST EDITION

ISBN   978-1-5445-3525-8 *Paperback*
        978-1-5445-3524-1 *Ebook*

To Dixie, for letting me love her.

To Dennette, for everything.

But especially for loving me.

(Thanks for saving me from killing myself. Good call!)

CONTENTS

PART TWO: THE ROADMAP

PART THREE: POINT B: BACK

INTRODUCTION, OR PREAMBLE, OR WHATEVER

Hey. So...a lot of people told me to write a book over the years. This is the book. You should probably buy it. Certainly read it, anyway. It's about my lifetime struggle with mental illness, how I didn't kill myself and learned to enjoy life. And how you can too.

It's a collection of stuff I wrote to help hurting people. This advice has helped dozens of men and women stuck in the same place I was: lonely, angry, numb, hopeless. It's saved lives. If it can show dozens how to get better, it can show thousands.

I've been diagnosed with treatment-resistant complex post-traumatic stress disorder (PTSD), clinical depression, a mood disorder, and generalized anxiety disorder. I'm an alcoholic. My wife of over twenty years died after a two-year losing battle with her own mental illness.

I went completely insane. But I had a new wife and a baby, so I couldn't kill myself. Everything I did to recover is in here.

I wrote it for a specific audience. You. Regardless of gender, ethnicity, orientation, or other label. Pain ignores demographic boundaries. So do I. Pain is broadly ecumenical. So's this book. It's written how I talk. Blunt, often vulgar, sometimes sarcastic, always honest, and from a place of deep caring.

I state psychological truths in here as I know them. I had to learn how my brain worked, and why, to fix it. This's what I learned and how I fixed it. It'll show you how to heal you, how to help others heal, and maybe even help heal our needlessly divided society.

I was also writing emails to my sons for when they're old enough. In hope that they don't grow up mentally ill, as I did. I saw the two streams worked symbiotically, so I mixed them.

It's chaotic at times. So was my mind. Some days, I couldn't write a paragraph; some I could. I chose not to rewrite anything. They're the words of a man struggling to find his way through insanity from that time, sharing pain, expressing thoughts, learning truths. You'll journey with me from despair to joy (spoiler alert).

You'll read some shit more than once. When battling mental illness, it takes constant reinforcement to replace negative thought patterns. The illness lies to you relentlessly, from multiple angles, telling the same lies in new ways to make you feel like shit. Well, this book tells the truth, relentlessly, from multiple angles.

Not everyone's a linguistic learner. Some folks don't like reading, and this works well for them. It's short, easily digestible chunks of information with advice delivered from different angles, driving the lessons home. I suggest reading each bit and thinking about it awhile, or going back and doing that after reading the whole thing. It's all connected. Like our brains. Like each other.

Some of this shit may anger you. A lot, probably everything, you're gonna read'll make you uncomfortable. You'll learn shit you've either been lied to about or hidden from your entire life. That kinda thing causes cognitive dissonance (we'll visit that later).

If you disagree with anything I've written, look it up. Educate yourself. Doubt everything and verify. Caveat: Google isn't your friend; Google Scholar is. If these words help you, great. If they don't, well, I've done what I can. Rule 4. (You'll get that later.) But they will.

Some will try to politicize me or argue my shit on theological grounds. You can't. I despise all political ideologies and organized religions; they're all judgment, no matter what they espouse. The extreme left, extreme right, and extremely religious are flocks guarded by wolves. I include a bunch of shit about how we, as a society, got to this point of skyrocketing mental illness rates. Why it's happened, how to mitigate the damage now, and most importantly, how to stop it from spreading to the next generations.

Some of this shit may come across as vilifying my parents. My parents aren't villains. They're victims of the same factors that twisted and shattered my psyche into shards and splinters. Once

I cursed them for giving me unwanted life, but had I not existed, neither would my sons, and that would've been a crime against the universe. I'm grateful for my parents.

I realized a while back that none of the psychology books or papers I was reading went far enough. I'm Indigenous and we believe healing must address everything: the body, the mind, the soul, and the environment. So I had to explore everything that broke my brain. Genetics, history, the social-political-religious systems we live under, grief, trauma…fucking everything. So I did. Now you will too.

Finally, none of this is self-pitying bullshit. I wrote this shit because someone at the time needed to know it. You probably do too. If not, buy the book anyway. You know somebody who does. Give it to them. After you've read it. Y'know…just in case…

PART ONE

POINT A: THE BRINK

1

MELTDOWN

In which our hero first finds the courage to express vulnerability and embarks on a strange journey indeed.

So…last August I had a mini-meltdown. Maybe not mini.

I'd been fine for so long.

And then I wasn't. Like, I really wasn't.

Uncontrollable rage. Uncontrollable weeping. Again.

It was like the bad times, before the therapy and before the meds.

The anxiety was back; the depression was back; the rage was back.

And I was right back in that place.

Makeitstopmakeitstopmakeitstopohgodspleasemakeitstop-whywon'titstopmakeitstop.

Some of you're asking why I'm telling y'all now. Why didn't I reach out then?

Because that's not how it works.

When you're there, you can't tell anyone. Because nobody'd ever understand.

You're all alone in the world.

And some are asking why I'm telling anybody at all.

Because I know my friends. Some of you know somebody like me.

Some of you are somebody like me.

Y'see, I went back to work.

On me.

Talked to some professionals, and we made a plan.

That plan included changing my meds a bit.

Just a tweak. Now, I'm, maybe for the first time ever, calm.

In control.

Stable.

I was worried I was just snowed. Which I would've put up with to not be a raging psycho around my kids. But I'm not.

Solid As in my university classes. (Oh yeah. I was stable enough to attend university. Surrounded by strangers in a strange place.)

But here's the thing: I'm a dad.

For the first time in my kids' lives, I feel that thing I always knew I was missing.

I can actually enjoy—cherish—my kids.

I guess I'm just sayin' if you're feeling alone in the darkness, you're not. If you're tired of being psychotically angry or numb and not knowing what's going on, if you think you can't get out of it, reach out. I know the way out.

Hell, I've had to find it twice now.

2

TRAUMA 101

In which our hero explains the science of trauma.

Why does a person experience something as traumatizing? Why does one person experience something as traumatizing when another person experiences the same thing without suffering any trauma? Why am I perfectly comfortable in life-threatening situations involving physical danger and violence but absolutely freaked out every time my child cries? Well, it's all about our ability to stay out of the fight/flight/freeze/flop response and stay engaged in the present moment. (I'll explain that in more depth in a sec.) There are several factors that influence our ability to do this, and most are a result of our previous experiences and consequent programming.

If a childhood threat, physical or emotional, was constantly present, we can (but will not necessarily) become traumatized. For life, unless we do work to deal with it. And we can only do work if we know it's there and choose to accept it. If we do have childhood trauma from abuse, neglect, or anything that causes us to live in fear and uncertainty, a trauma response becomes much more likely in how we're liable to react to a new threat, real or imagined.

Our past determines how we're likely to respond to current events. Our brain draws from past experiences to understand current ones, and everything goes through our amygdala first, to let it scan for threats. The amygdala remembers scary things. We developed it to protect ourselves from predators. Our amygdala recognizes threat patterns. (Hmmm…I see a bush moving, I smell a cat, I hear a growl, HolyFuckingShit! Sabretooth!!!!)

But our most primary emotions are stored here, too, so we see everything through an emotional lens before the rational part of our brain even gets involved. If we experience something potentially traumatic and have nothing in our past for our brain to connect it with, our subconscious tries to force connections that don't work, and we get weird daydreams and nightmares while our subconscious tries to process shit.

Memories of trauma are stored in a different part of the brain than where normal memories are stored. Traumatic memory is stored in the limbic part of the brain, not the temporal cortex. Scary events get stored in our most primitive part of the brain because it's about survival, first of the individual, then of the species. The limbic system exists to help us instinctively survive danger. But it can't differentiate between actual physical threats and emotional threats. It reacts to both the same way. My brain would freak out over being "disrespected" by my wife way more than it would to a physical danger. Physical danger I could fight. Purely imaginary threats to my sense of self, now…

Why are traumatic memories stored in the limbic system?

Probably because they're too painful and overwhelming for the conscious mind to focus past regularly. They take up all of our brainpower as it is. But they're remembered, unwillingly and unknowingly, through triggers. Triggers bring up the memory from our limbic system, and we experience it, emotionally, as an event occurring in the present. The threat is right now, even though the current situation has nothing to do with any threat at all! We basically imagine a threat and react to it.

Triggers shoot us way past our nervous system's Window of Tolerance (our ability to stay present in the reality we share). As soon as we leave the window, our nervous system goes into hyper- or hypo-arousal and we re-experience the fear right now. Except...except there is no threat, and we're still trapped there...in the fear of our past.

Attachment style also plays a huge role in our ability to cope with traumatic events and our responses to new stimuli, threatening or not, later in life. Our attachment style is a way of describing how we relate to the other people in our various relationships. Our attachment style is the emotional bond that forms between children and their caregivers. It's created and influenced in infancy and early childhood as a response to how our earliest caregivers react to our needs. Attachment gives the infant its first coping mechanism and creates the baby's social development, while also shaping its emotional and cognitive development. Attachment encourages brain growth and development.

Our attachment style progresses and matures through the baby's daily routine, as its caregivers either attend to or ignore its various needs. If the caregivers are always attending to the baby when it cries, it develops healthier attachment styles. If the child grows in an environment where it normally receives the care it requires, the child continues to develop healthier attachment styles.

Attachment style has a long-lasting effect on how we form and maintain relationships. Basically, our adult attachment style duplicates the relationship we had with our primary caregivers when we were infants and children. I read one paper where neuroscientists believed oxytocin developed either because of or to create secure attachment, and the brain has developed entire networks of neurons dedicated to it because it's such a primitive and primary function. I ain't gonna argue with neuroscientists about neuroscience.

People with secure attachment generally have more and/or better emotional and intellectual resources to deal with shitty events. Apparently, attachment styles can change over time and from relationship to relationship. Enduring a terrible relationship might lead to a less secure attachment orientation; it's harder to remain securely attached to a partner who's unfaithful or violent, for instance. A supportive relationship may lead to increased security, even if we grew up in a home where we had insecure attachments with our primary caregivers. If you're all kinds of fucked up, like I was, in regard to attachment, therapy can be immensely helpful. Therapy can provide a safe connection to another human and give us an opportunity to learn better relational skills than we learned in our childhood.

3

TO MY SONS #1

In which our hero realizes the advice to his sons aimed at preventing mental illness and his advice to the mentally ill on how to heal are symbiotic.

My sons, we're in chaotic times, and everyone around us is afraid. I'm not.

The runes of our lives were carved long years before you were a gleam in your great-great-great-great-great-grandfather's eye. You'll live as long as you're supposed to and die when it's appointed.

Hide in a hole in a cave and it'll change nothing.

It doesn't matter how long you live. What matters is how you live.

It doesn't matter when you die; it matters how you are spoken of when you do.

Live bravely and you'll fail often, but your successes will be great. Live bravely and you'll live without regret.

Speak the truth. Keep your word. Work hard. Help those you can.

Do these things and you'll feel no shame when you die.

Find the courage to be kind. Be strong enough to be compassionate.

These things will ensure you're remembered with honour.

Any coward can hate. Any weakling can be selfish.

These things will ensure you're remembered with disdain.

Dedicate yourself to your values, not to your possessions. You'll only take the one to the next life.

Do more than exist, my sons: live. Concern yourself with the life in your lifetime, and don't worry about the time.

This is a thing I've learned: it's not about who you are. It's about who you want to be.

It's not about what you've done or where you've been. It's about what you want to achieve.

Figure out who you want to be. Then be that person.

If you don't know how, do what I did: fake it. If you try to do the things that person would, you'll eventually always do those things.

If you try to act like that person would act, eventually you'll always act that way.

If you want to be brave, do brave things. If you want to be kind, do kind things.

And then, one day, you are that person.

So…who do you want to be? I love you.

4

SUICIDE

In which our hero speaks about suicide in hopes of preventing it.

I thought about killing myself. Three times in my life.

I've been sitting in front of this screen for I don't know how long trying to find the parts to say that.

I've hinted at it in previous posts, but I've never flat-out said it, I don't think. It's hard. What'll people think? What'll this do to my parents? Blah, blah, blah. All kinds of excuses to not cowboy up and speak truth. But here I am, crying and typing. Please excuse any typos.

The first time was a long time ago. When I was a teenager. Yeah, I've been dancing this dance a long time. Probably my entire life. The second time was when Dixie, my first wife, died. My universe was gone. I wasn't a soldier anymore, and the centre of my world was gone. So, fuck it. Then Dennette, my current wife, exploded into my life and took it over. She's why I didn't go through with it...then.

The last time was a few years ago. The anxiety attacks were in full control, and I couldn't see any other way out. Y'see, for those you who've never been there, when you get to that point, it actually makes sense. It's logical. It ends the pain, and it makes life better for my loved ones to not have to worry about me. I'm just a burden to them anyway. Yeah, that's what your brain does to you when you get that far.

So don't. If you're struggling, get help. Right now. Call someone. Right now. Now.

But Dennette saved me again. She saved me because she'd given me my son, and he needed his daddy. Crazy or not, I still knew he needed a daddy. So I reached out. Took some time off work and started seriously working on therapy. Like, hard. For my son.

I shoulda died a few times other than that, y'know. Shoulda died on tours a couple times. Didn't. Shoulda died parachuting twice. Didn't. Shoulda died drinking a couple times. Didn't.

The only reason I can think I'm still here, well, two reasons, I think: (1) to make my sons; (2) to tell people. To find the ones who're suffering and hurting and struggling and tell them my story. So they know they aren't alone. None of us are alone.

That's what I do now: tell kids. Meeting kids who tell me about their demons. Kids who message me or text me or whatever. They're where I find the parts to cowboy up. Because they need me, just as much as my children. They need to hear this.

If you're not the one struggling, but you love someone who is, you can talk to me too. For perspective. For knowledge. To cry with or yell at, because you can't yell at them, or whatever you need to do.

Pain is pain. Watching someone hurt, hurts. I know that. I lived it. I see it in Dennette's face when I go dark. But she stays. I put her through hell, and she stays. So if you're like me, I'm here to listen. If you're like Dennette, and love someone who's hurting, I'm here to listen.

Please share this. It took a lot of effort to write, and it might be exactly what someone else, someone I can't reach, needs. Thanks for listening.

5

FAILED COPING MECHANISMS #1

In which our hero breaks trauma response down scientifically.

People struggling with mental illness use a number of coping mechanisms to "control" trauma response. They all work great until they all fail miserably and shit gets real fucking bad, real fucking quick. Trust me. Below are some of the failed coping mechanisms traumatized people may use. I've done all this shit at one point or another.

Repression is unconscious and not unconscious at the same time. Pretty weird. We don't want to think about shit, so we force ourselves to forget it. We block emotions and memories we don't want to remember.

Denial is, well, it's fucking denial. It's flat-out refusing to accept reality we don't like, even when faced with overwhelming evidence. Some people get so into this they actually, literally, don't see shit they should see or hear shit they should hear.

Repression isn't denial, but they work sorta the same and sometimes together. Denial reacts to external stuff we don't want to accept; repression reacts to mental stuff we don't want to accept. Denial is external; repression is internal.

Displacement is redirecting our feelings from their legit target to something safer. (Classic example: guy has a bad day at work, bottles it all up, then takes it out on his wife.) People struggling with depression or suicidal ideation often displace our feelings by redirecting anger for others onto ourselves.

Dissociation is remembering or thinking about shit without allowing ourselves to experience the emotions we probably should. Dissociation is quite common, and you see it a lot with vets and inmates, when they start joking about really bad shit or go into the thousand-yard stare and start talking about horrible shit without any emotion. Really serious forms of dissociation can be loss of consciousness or entering a different level of consciousness or amnesia. I have, on two occasions, gone into a bizarre sort of trance that has terrified Dennette. I just sort of... left...mentally went away, apparently. I don't really recall much.

Projection is transferring unacceptable emotions or thoughts onto others: "I'm not paranoid; I'm a realist. You're paranoid." And "I'm not scared; I'm angry. You're scared." Projection is pure distrust, pure fear, usually of judgment. Someone trying to hide behind projection is always watching for proof their fears are correct. We isolate and can't build or maintain relationships because we're overly touchy about petty shit so we can feel humiliated, therefore holding a grudge until the end of days.

Rationalization means using feeble arguments to blow by

shit we don't want to admit to. The number of times I've self-sabotaged, then rationalized it away...sitting here, I'm watching a movie of stupid moments go by. Here's the thing: we're not rational creatures. None of us. We're rationalizing creatures. Remember, everything goes through the amygdala first. We emotionally experience it, get triggered, do something stupid out of anxiety, and then rationalize it so we can pretend we're rational. Totally irrational behaviour.

Reaction formation is when we act in ways that are diametrically opposed to our actual thoughts and feelings, but not deliberately. Like when I'm homicidally angry (from some imagined slight my anxiety has interpreted as a threat to my survival—insert rolly-eyes-emoji-thing here), I hold my body perfectly still and talk in a ridiculously over-the-top calm voice, using multiple polysyllabic words in each sentence and being more polite than a Victorian earl. Another example is my being scared to death all the time but considering this cowardice, not anxiety, so I overcompensated with overly masculine bull-shit. On the bright side, I have some wicked tattoos from that. (Thanks, Yura!)

Splitting is dividing people into "good" and "bad" by seeing just positive or negative qualities. Instead of accepting humans are a complex mixture of emotions and behaviours, we split them into groups, either friend or foe. It's easier for our limbic system to deal with them that way. It requires less thought and allows us to react to them on an emotional level, but with a very small and tightly controlled set of emotions. Because the amygdala only accesses a very small and tightly controlled set of emotions.

Howwwwever...as Dennette can attest (I'm so fucking sorry,

baby)…this idea of black and white means our shit can reverse in a goddamn instant, and the people closest to us can be the very personification of all that is virtuous one second, then immediately become the personification of all that is evil the next, if our crazy decides that's more convenient than actually confronting reality and accepting some blame for our own shit. Splitting was really bad with me for a while, when I was completely emotionally unstable following Dixie's death. I had absolutely zero sense of my own identity, having lost the idea of being "Dixie's husband," and my grief was alternating with a sense of being abandoned.

Deflection is a means to prevent having attention brought to you, either blame or acclaim, depending on your personal sense of worth and fear of judgment. I've had very little of the former and way too much of the latter for most of my life. I've seldom feared blame, although I can recall an instance on my junior leadership course when my master corporal asked me where my web gear was, and when I opened my mouth to answer, someone else's voice came out and lied to him. Sooo, I'm sure it's happened more than once. To my eternal shame, the man I lied to was a personal hero and friend. (Shorty, I miss you every day.) My deflecting has usually been to avoid positive attention. I remember having (what I now recognize as) an anxiety attack when my company leadership was going to put my name forward for the top soldier of the brigade. I got them to quash the nomination.

We (mentally ill folks, that is) find it frightening and painful to think rationally about change. Thinking we might need to change threatens the beliefs (rational and irrational alike) we use to create our sense of identity. This sense of self, remember, is created in the first seven years of our life and is always seen through the lens of the amygdala. We aren't going to change everything overnight. That's like trying to turn the *Titanic* 180 degrees on a dime. A giant change in someone's mentality or outlook on life or sense of self or whatever the fuck you wanna call it, is probably gonna be negative, a drop so severe it smashes through the coping mechanisms they've been trying to use and sends them spiralling into depression. Ask me how I know. Then, to reverse that, it takes serious fucking effort over time, incrementally making tiny steps forward for what seems like forever, until you make a big breakthrough. Again, ask me how I know.

But it's clearly doable, cuz I done it. You can too.

6

COGNITIVE DISSONANCE

In which our hero explains why we do stupid shit.

Why is it such a struggle to admit our shit to ourselves? Our family, our friends, our doctors, our shrinks, our whoever can tell us we're doing really dumb shit and sometimes we even believe them, but usually not. Why? We can be ruining our every relationship, losing work, becoming physically unhealthier, abusing substances…all kinds of harmful things, and we still insist on continuing the shit we're doing to destroy our lives. Why?

Once we admit to ourselves a behaviour is irrational, we start trying to stop it. But getting there takes months or years or decades of heartbreak. Why? Especially considering how much relief we feel each time we do it, why?

Because we literally couldn't. Because of cognitive dissonance and all the failed coping mechanisms we talked about earlier: repression, denial, rationalization. What's cognitive dissonance?

It's when our brain tries to believe two mutually opposing thoughts simultaneously. In simple terms (because I'm a simple man), it's like trying to believe up really is up while knowing up is down. I was trying to believe two totally opposite things at the same time.

My rational brain knew one thing to be true and factual, but my irrational mind believed something altogether different. For instance, my lucid mind knew my wife and her family wanted to take a cute generational family photo, but my irrational mind saw it as a threat to my very being. True story. You should see the pictures. I look like I'm psychotic with rage. Because I was. Over a family photo.

You can't connect reality with your perception of reality. Your brain tries to resolve the dissonance using failed coping mechanisms. You repress the stuff you literally can't accept you've done, deny the stuff you don't want to see, and rationalize the rest. You displace your anger at your parents onto yourself because that's what children do. (Kids are totally self-centred, so anything that happens is their fault. That's why kids of divorces can be messed up sometimes.) You displace your self-anger on others when they confront you with reality. You use projection to constantly punish yourself.

To get the dissonance to end, we have to make ourselves change thought patterns we already have (patterns that might've been programmed into us from infancy, FYI, so that's a bitch); add new thought patterns or ideas to pre-existing thought patterns (I found this the easiest of the three, personally); and/or make previous thought patterns and beliefs less important to us, letting go of the idea we must be correct or our whole world will end.

When you successfully involve the temporal cortex, cerebral cortex, prefrontal cortex, and limbic system, you end the dissonance. That's what processing is. You accept reality and stop using failed coping mechanisms. That's what therapy work is. And that's why you can't fix your shit by yourself. You can't even see it. You think the problem is X, when it's actually Y and Z. Get help. For real.

7

TO MY SONS #2

In which our hero gives advice to prevent insecurity and shame from taking root.

My sons, stand for what you believe in, even if you must stand alone. Die standing rather than live kneeling. Persistence and tenacity are priceless. Lions and tigers look fierce, but neither wolverines nor badgers perform in circuses, and nuthin' is more tenacious than those buggers.

Hard work betrays no one. Success is never guaranteed. You may work hard and still fail. The harder you work, the more likely you'll succeed. Should you not, you'll have learned. If nothing else, you've learned a way not to do something.

People feel they're owed something from the world. They're wrong. We're owed nothing. You were given life; do something with it. Work hard. Today's the opportunity to be better than you were yesterday.

Be who you are, not who you think someone else (including

me) wants you to be. Authenticity is rare, and rarity creates value. Be real. Real recognizes real, and only real people are worth having in your life.

People say violence never solves anything. Punch them in the mouth; prove them wrong when they shut up. Violence in self-defence is, of course, necessary. Gautama Buddha and Jesus of Nazareth both said so, and they were pretty pacifistic, as I recall. Violence is rarely the best option. But when required, it's the only option. A good man isn't a man who fears to fight. A good man is one who controls his violence until needed.

Some people claim they're morally opposed to violence. They lie. They fear violence. They're protected by those of us who overcome fear. Courage isn't lack of fear. It's doing what you must despite fear. We cannot be brave until, first, we're scared. If you find yourself afraid, it means you're confronted with the opportunity to be courageous.

Don't pray for easy times. Make yourself strong enough, wise enough, adaptable enough to thrive in difficult ones. Tough times give us the opportunity to become tough. Crying, vomiting, swearing…all are acceptable. Quitting isn't. Nothing worth having comes easy. Nothing that comes easy is worth having.

Be kind. Kindness isn't weakness. Being kind can be difficult. Sometimes the kindest thing you can do for someone is to punch them in the mouth. There'll be times you need a punch in the mouth. Be grateful when you get it. It'll make you a better man.

Embrace the suck. Complacency is stagnation. Stagnation is a living death. Live, don't exist. Remember, above all, I love you.

8

ATTACHMENT #1

In which our hero explains how earliest childhood can set up later mental illness.

Infants and children need a reliable, attentive caregiver in their lives to form secure attachments. If an infant or child doesn't have a dependable, supportive caregiver in their life, they develop an insecure attachment style that carries over into adulthood. Basically, the theory says our behaviour in adult relationships replicates the behaviour we learned in our infancy and childhood from our caregivers.

There are a few (four, in most things I've read on the subject) different attachment styles. They're Secure Attachment (the good one), Avoidant Attachment, Anxious Attachment, and Disorganized Attachment (a blend of Avoidant and Anxious). I'm gonna talk about the two negative ones (Avoidant and Anxious) that have impacted my life. Because I or someone I loved was labouring under them, they're the only ones I know enough about to speak on with confidence.

Avoidant Attachment creates a fear of intimacy and trusting others. Avoidant Attachment styles come about because of an insecure attachment to caregivers in infancy and childhood, and the child learns not to trust because their caregiver isn't always available. So they armour up their emotions. Wall everything up. Build a fortress that can't be penetrated. If you don't trust, you can't be let down, so you can't be hurt. Avoidant Attachment people have a real tough time dealing with the difficult emotions, so they don't. They use repression and denial a lot. They tend to have lots of short-lived relationships. If they bail first, they can't be abandoned. So they maintain an emotional unavailability, and real relationships make them feel trapped or suffocated. Avoidant Attachment people subconsciously push their partner away to create the failed relationship they know will happen. All relationships have an expiry date to them.

Anxious Attachment people (Hello, my name is Sheridan, and I'm Anxious Attachment) have a fear of intimacy and trusting others but desperately want intimacy and the trust of others. It's a bitch. Let's see the checklist, shall we?

1. No self-worth and poor self-esteem. Check!
2. Always wanting reassurance, approval, or validation from a partner. Check!
3. Always looking for any signs of problems in the relationship. Check!
4. Extremely impulsive and highly emotional. Check!
5. Mood swings and/or wildly unpredictable emotional reactions to relationship problems. Check!

Yeesh! I feel like a whiner reading that, but there it is. If the caregiver in the child's life is emotionally or physically unavailable and doesn't always respond to a child's needs, the child can develop a fear of being abandoned. So, yeah, it's a bitch for both partners because the Anxious Attachment one comes across as super needy and clingy.

We learn from our past and repeat past behaviours, even negative ones. Likewise, we recreate past relationships, even ones filled with insecurity, fear, infidelity, or violence. Shitty relationships with a caregiver cause us to recreate the same relationship with partners. It's our normal and the way a relationship is supposed to go! Or maybe we deserve a shitty relationship because we're unworthy of love, so we choose shitty partners or subconsciously poison a relationship to create a self-fulfilling prophecy. Genius, no? Or maybe we choose a shitty partner because they remind us of Mommy or Daddy, and it's our last shot at getting Mommy or Daddy to love us. How messed up does that make you feel?

9

MEDICATION

In which our hero talks about his meds to encourage those needing medication.

So…let's talk about medication.

Took me a long time to swallow my pride and see I needed chemical help to stabilize my out-of-control emotions.

Big part of that was the anxiety trying to keep me from getting better. I picture my crazy (my therapist hates it when I use that word) as a living thing inside my brain. I imagine it trying to survive by working against the rational part.

Bigger part, I think, was my ego. "I don't need anything. I got this. I'm (here comes that bullshit stigma) not weak."

I had to put my wife and kid through absolute hell before I cowboyed up.

I had to get to the point of complete desperation before I found the parts to tell my doctor, "I need meds."

And it's so stupid!

Got a headache, take an Aspirin and get some rest.

Got an infection, take antibiotics and get some rest.

Got a cold, take some cold meds and get some rest.

Got a serotonin deficiency, take an antidepressant and get some therapy.

I was so stupid for so long. It's so obvious!

Now.

Now the meds are helping me regulate my emotions.

Depression isn't weakness. Anxiety isn't weakness. Trauma isn't weakness. They're medical conditions. So taking medication for a medical condition is just logical.

It's hard to be logical when you're dark. Almost impossible.

I'm not saying meds are the solution. But they're a part of it for me.

The therapy couldn't work because the anxiety wouldn't let it. Calm the anxiety, and the therapy could do its thing. But even with the therapy working, it still wasn't enough.

I needed to tweak my meds to stabilize. I might be on them forever. I'm good with that. Life is good now. I experience emotions at a level that is appropriate now.

I'm not saying everybody who's hurting needs meds. But they're an option.

Maybe you should explore it, if your medical professional suggests it.

The hardest stuff is the stuff most worth doing.

10

WINDOW OF
TOLERANCE

In which our hero explains how the body's responses to stress can create mental illness.

First, you need to open a new tab and look up Window of Tolerance so you've a picture to work with. Should be lots. Okay, got it? Or I guess you could just look at a real fucking window, huh? Anyway…this theory was developed by a guy named Dan Siegel, and I learned it in veterans' group therapy.

Everybody has a mental arousal range in which we best process information and function through the day. That's the "window." Stress management is optimal, and we can cope with the various problems, physical or mental, as they come without too much hindrance. The top and bottom sills of the window are our max stress-tolerance boundaries. Beyond…there be dragons.

If we go beyond the top sill, we enter a hyperarousal state: fight-or-flight reactions. For me, that meant years of anxiety attacks, fear, hypervigilance, emotional flooding, and dissociative rage. Fight-or-flight mode for hours, days, weeks at a time with no emotional regulation ability at all. Sheer rage and always prepared for violence.

But the human brain can only tolerate so much hyperarousal before getting overwhelmed, shutting down, and numbing out. This is hypo-arousal. My system would shut off, and I'd be trapped in depression. Just go flat. No emotions at all. Unable to function sometimes, often I'd have no appetite for weeks, wouldn't shower for days, couldn't make a decision or remember what I was doing from moment to moment.

But the human brain can only stay in shutdown mode for so long before it wants to feel "alive" again. This leads to hyperarousal, which leads to hypo-arousal, and my life was a roller coaster of extreme ups and downs. This can mean a wide variety of out-of-character, high-risk behaviour, like drinking, doing drugs, gambling, or cheating, depending on various factors. I did some shit I'm deeply ashamed of and may never really know if that was me being an asshole or my anxiety making me be an asshole.

Right, science...trauma and unmet childhood attachment needs shrink our Window of Tolerance. They dramatically screw up our emotional regulation ability. This means I'd get completely overwhelmed by shitty events and negative emotions more quickly, or I'd magnify mildly negative events into catastrophes that then overwhelmed me. My negative experiences and emotional reactions were uncontrollably intense, and I'd never learned healthy coping mechanisms. Even if I had, though, when above or below the window sills, coping mechanisms are less accessible to even a stable mind.

I always knew something was very wrong somewhere, but I didn't know what or why. Because I hadn't formed healthy attachment bonds in infancy or learned emotional regulation in childhood, any traumas stayed in my brain, trapping my emotional self in early childhood. A six-foot, 210-pound toddler having tantrums. I didn't know how to regulate my emotions and couldn't manage their intensity, so I'd try to use failed coping mechanisms until they'd explode and take control. Then all hell would break loose.

11

"I'M JUST..."

In which our hero supports those who feel judged for having a mental illness.

I don't like it when people attribute my shit only to PTSD and my military service. Here's why: it's an attempt to quantify and limit mental illness, and it perpetuates the stigma.

It belittles and demeans the struggles of others who haven't served.

It sends this message of "It's acceptable for that person to battle mental illness."

And that sends the wrong message. People with mental illness start to think, "Nothing bad happened to me, so I'm just..." It's the "I'm just..." that we need to fight.

What about the nurse in the maternity ward who has to handle ill and dead infants on a regular basis? Is it okay for them to have some shit going on?

Or the kid born into a family of substance, verbal, mental, physical, or sexual abuse? Is it okay for them?

Or the teenager who actually has a pretty stable life but inherited the wrong gene and their brain chemistry goes wonky? Is it okay for them?

You see what I mean?

I work with some trauma groups. I see this stupid stigma all the time: I wasn't military; I shouldn't be struggling. I wasn't Army; I shouldn't be struggling. I wasn't infantry; I shouldn't be struggling. I didn't deploy; I shouldn't be struggling. I didn't deploy to [insert country]; I shouldn't be struggling.

There is no tier system to pain!

Pain is pain. Hurt is hurt. Depression sucks. Anxiety sucks.

"Why" is only relevant to the suffering person and their therapist so they can figure out how to work on it.

For the rest of us, it's way more simple.

Give them love.

12

JOHARI WINDOW #1

In which our hero explains why connection is vital for mental health.

I learned about the Johari window in veterans' group therapy. It's called the Johari window because it was invented by two dudes named Joe and Harry. Get it? (Okay, I looked it up; psychologists Joseph Luft and Harrington Ingham invented it.)

Right, so either look it up in a new tab for an image, or just look at a window divided into quarters. Whichever. We use the Johari window as a method to imagine ourselves and how we can better increase our understanding of ourselves. It's divided into four panes: Open, Blind Spot, Hidden, and Unknown. (If it makes you feel better, you can say that last one in a spooky Bela Lugosi voice.)

The Open pane is the information about ourselves that we, and other people, know about us. The Open pane is enlarged by reducing the Hidden and Unknown panes through displaying vulnerability and receiving non-judgmental feedback. We increase the Open pane and decrease the Blind Spot pane as we learn about ourselves from other people.

The Blind Spot pane is the information other people know about us, but we don't. Other people see us differently, or maybe more accurately, than we do because we spend all our time lying to ourselves, and they see things about us we can't. This is why I can see your shit, but you can't, and vice versa. The stuff we don't see about ourselves isn't necessarily bad, either. We very often blind ourselves to our good attributes, especially when lost in mental illness. The Blind Spot pane is reduced by receiving non-judgmental and accurate feedback.

The Hidden pane is the information about ourselves known to us that we keep unknown to other people. We all keep some information as private as we can, usually something we're ashamed of or otherwise fear judgment for. Secrets of any kind are seldom helpful or healthy. The Hidden pane has to be reduced by revealing this private information to the Open pane by finding the courage to be vulnerable and sharing it. When you're bananas, that's way easier said than done. But I suggest to you, if you're hiding secrets from people, how can you have healthy relationships? If you don't have healthy relationships, can you be emotionally healthy?

The Unknown pane is the information about ourselves everyone is unaware of, us included. This can be due to traumatic experiences, mental illness, or attachment issues. This information can be locked in the Unknown pane for our entire lifetime. Sometimes we discover it ourselves somehow, but it most often happens as we open up to other people, if we choose to hear them.

The Johari window model helps explain why we, as humans, need to voluntarily reveal information about ourselves to other people in order to increase our understanding of ourselves. We learn about ourselves from listening to them. Using the model, information moves from Unknown panes to known panes as connection is gained through vulnerability and non-judgmental feedback. The larger the Open pane becomes, the better our relationships become. The better our relationships get, the better our lives get and the more emotionally stable we are. Connection is how we heal mental injuries and emotional wounds. These injuries and wounds might be invisible, but they're every bit as painful and debilitating as physical ones. The more we learn about ourselves, the more we overcome our fear of judgment, the more control we develop over our emotional responses, and the better we can regulate.

Y'know, I bet there's some sort of animated thingie on the net about this somewhere. Coulda saved a shit-ton of typing. Fuck me...

13

ATTACHMENT #2

In which our hero explains attachment further so readers can improve relationships.

An Avoidant person denies attachment needs and suppresses attachment-related thoughts and emotions ("dealing but not feeling"). They distrust partners and try to maintain emotional independence and distance. They show compulsive self-reliance, refusing to receive from or give to others. They want a relationship but feel trapped by intimacy. Essentially, they avoid getting too close for fear of losing their partners.

Research identified two types of Avoidant Attachment: Fearful and Dismissive. The Fearful Avoidant hopes to eventually connect yet fears connection and pulls away. The Dismissive Avoidant person will be commitment-phobic and use small imperfections in the partner as an excuse for not getting too involved. They purposely distance themselves by acting ambivalently, openly flirting with others, cheating, not communicating their thoughts or feelings, or staying out of touch for days or weeks after an intimate encounter.

Those who develop Avoidant Attachment learned to inhibit emotion and dissociate from the body. They have underdeveloped socio-emotional intelligence, as early environments gave little opportunity for growing it. They minimize emotional needs and crawl into their heads, staying there to survive their family environment. As adults, they come off as dismissive of others and of relationships. They have limited access to their emotions and deny their needs. They don't seek comfort from others; instead, they may be irritable and short-tempered with others.

Individuals with high levels of avoidance were less sexually satisfied in their marriages. Furthermore, those who had Avoidant partners were also less sexually satisfied. Avoidant individuals fail to associate sexual behaviour with intimacy and are more likely to have casual, noncommittal sexual relationships than committed relationships.

The Anxious Attachment style is always concerned about the stability or security of the relationship. People with this attachment style tend to agonize over the meaning of words or actions by a partner. They read negatives into otherwise neutral or positive interactions. They also tend to crave constant reassurance the relationship is secure and the affection and love are still present.

The specifics of how an attachment style develops can be linked to different factors. With the Anxious Attachment style, the most common factor is inconsistency in parenting. This may be related to parents that respond with excessive love and attention sometimes, while failing to respond at others.

Relationships with these individuals are often very stressful, with the partner feeling crowded or smothered in the relationship, while continually needing to provide positive feedback to the individual with the Anxious Attachment style.

14

THE RULES

In which our hero first explains the Rules he learned to keep us mentally healthy.

To my sons: every man wishes to pass along great wisdom to his children, as well as the less important, material things in life. This is the greatest wisdom I have, and if you heed my words, your life will be immeasurably improved thereby. Live according to the Rules. The Rules will keep you from shame. Shame destroys your mind and your soul. It has no benefit. I've spent decades finding the right code to live by, and it's only through a lifetime of shame and sorrow that I've discovered the Rules. I would spare you my mistakes and my pain.

The Rules

1. Speak the truth.
2. Keep your word.
3. Work hard.
4. Help those you can.

The first rule is first because it's the most important. If you strive to only ever speak the truth, you cannot lie. You choose your words with great care. If you cannot lie, then you cannot do things you'd be ashamed of. If you cannot lie, then you never have secrets to hide from those you love. Secrets are never beneficial between people who love one another. They're toxic to relationships and toxic to your soul. They weaken the mind and poison your every thought. You live in fear. Fear of discovery. Fear of judgment. Live your life openly and honestly, and you have no fear, for you have no secrets.

Speak the truth; it requires courage and discipline, and neither of these qualities has failed a man. Speak the truth. It's simple; it's rarely easy; it's always necessary. The truth can hurt another, but never so much as betrayal. I cannot think of anything I've done that causes me as much shame as my betrayal of others, for I cannot think of anything I've done that has hurt another so badly.

The second rule is very similar to the first and is only marginally less important. They're symbiotic in nature. They must go hand in hand. They're separate rules, however, because a clever man (and you're both too clever by far already) can find the semantics he needs to abide by the one rule and yet not obey the second. I know. I'm a clever man. And failing to do as I've said has shamed me.

The measure of a man can be taken by the regard in which he's held by those who observe him. If a man is believed to be trustworthy by those who know him, their respect for him is immeasurable. Fame is fleeting and a harsh mistress. Fortune causes envy and therefore spite. Athleticism and beauty fade.

Respect is eternal. We're immortal if we live on in the memories of those we leave behind. Choose how you would be remembered. Do those who think of you, today and a century from now, think of you as a man they'd loan money to with only a handshake?

And how do you think of yourself? If you're unreliable, you've no regard for others. If you don't keep your word to them, you're saying, "you don't matter to me." Our reputation among others, those we value, dictates how we think of ourselves. Do nothing that'll cause others to think less of you, for you'll do the same.

If you strive to only speak the truth and always keep your word, you cannot lie and you choose your words with great care. Words are more than air passing through our teeth. They're thoughts. They're who we are. Nothing can happen without the thought becoming word, to become deed. Choose your words with care. Waste none. Use only those you intend to abide by.

These rules keep you from secrecy. Shame grows in secrecy. It feeds upon deception. Secrets and lies only make shame stronger. Dishonour will stain your soul and break your mind. Be honest, be trustworthy, and you cannot have secrets or tell lies. Shame cannot plant itself in your soul. Secrets and lies trap you in a web that only gets more complicated and stronger, binding you in ties of pain and sorrow.

Rule 3 is so much more than two words. If you would do a thing, anything, do it to the best of your ability, always, or don't do it at all. Whether that thing be your employment, your hobby, or a menial task you resent is irrelevant. Do it to the best of your ability.

When you do anything to your best effort, you take pride in it. You take pride in the attempt. You take pride in your efforts. You take pride in yourself. When we know we could've done better, we feel shame for not trying. This, then, leads to self-deception, which leads to outward lying and to secrets. And then we begin a long, slow spiral into becoming a man we wish we weren't. Self-loathing is shame; it's your brain saying to you, "I'm a bad person." If you put forward your best in all things, you cannot feel shame.

Failing isn't shameful. Poor effort is shameful. Not attempting something out of fear of failure is shameful. Doing things to our best ensures we'll always find the courage to attempt, to try, to fail, and thereby to learn. Poor effort leads to failure through lack of effort and becomes habitual. Better to fail grandly, and glory in the attempt, than to never attempt a thing at all. To never try is to exist, not to live. Seek challenge and try. Work hard.

Rule 4 is exactly as it says. Help those you can. You won't always have the means to help another, or they may not want your help. But every day you'll meet someone who needs help. Perhaps it's the single mother who cannot manage the groceries and the children. Perhaps it's the homeless person who hasn't eaten yet that day; perhaps it's someone who's battling an inner war you cannot see.

Every day, look for those who need your help and will accept it. Nothing defeats shame more effectively than being of service to others, putting forth your best effort for them, and having them see you're trustworthy and deserving of respect. Social acceptance—being seen, heard, and understood—allows connection and connection to others heals. Mental illness, addiction: these things always first seek to isolate us from others. Helping others ensures we cannot isolate and allows us to receive the social acceptance we crave.

Rule 4 means we cannot ignore those who need the same social acceptance we crave. Rule 4 ensures we do our very best at always being as good a person as we can. You cannot feel shame if you strive to help others. You cannot be ashamed of yourself if you are a good person.

Everywhere you go, you'll encounter rules, laws, regulations, taboos. Everywhere, other people will try to tell you how you must live. Be wary of others' rules. Very few people create rules for the betterment of others, and their rules are seldom wise. Most are ill-conceived, poorly thought out, and aimed at your expense, at limiting your growth. I'm your father, I love you, and my rules are aimed at your betterment. I discovered and designed them to keep me from shame, and they'll do the same for you. The Rules will make your life better, and I pass them on to you because I love you.

Learn the Rules, my sons. Do your best to live according to them. They'll give you the greatest success I can wish upon you. They'll make you people you are proud to be.

15

WINDOW OF TOLERANCE, THE SEQUEL

In which our hero further explains stress responses and connects them to shame.

The autonomic nervous system is divided into two parts: the sympathetic nervous system (SNS) and the parasympathetic nervous system (PNS). These two subsystems work without conscious direction from our brain (hence the name "autonomic," I suppose). The SNS is tied into the limbic system and controls the fight/flight/freeze/flop reaction. We have no control over it.

The PNS helps the body get back to normal following the fight-or-flight "adrenalin dump": slowed heart rate, blood circulation restored, no more tunnel vision, digestive system working, no more auditory exclusion. We do have some control over the PNS, as we can speed up the return to normal through breathing. That's why controlled breathing under stress works, whether the stress is caused by a physical threat or a psychological threat, such as trauma.

Training, particularly military training, teaches soldiers to function in the hyperarousal state because combat sends us there. We'd better be fucking prepared to function there. We stay in, and function at, a narrow range just below the top sill of the Window of Tolerance, just before we go into hypo-arousal, where we can't function at all anymore.

This means our window either narrows exponentially, or "moves up," where the top sill becomes the middle and the middle becomes the bottom sill. We're functioning at max capacity all the fucking time. Either way you want to look at it, our ability to deal with stress and recover from traumatic events is dramatically reduced. We've no psychological buffer zone anymore. We can't regulate effectively, and we can't ever reach a prior level of calm, as our new "normal" is "freaked the fuck out."

This is the classic case of PTSD. Hypervigilance. Rocketing between depression and anxiety attacks. Mysophobia. Agoraphobia. All the shit I struggle through. Why am I explaining this to you? Well, because…the exact same fucking thing happens to children who grow up with unattached caregivers, especially unattached caregivers and physical/verbal/psychological abuse. They don't necessarily have the same symptoms, but the same damage to the limbic system and the SNS results. Then add attachment issues onto it, and terrible things are just waiting to happen.

Now, shame also shrinks our window. But shame isn't only

caused by our actions. All too often, shame is put on us like a rucksack. Most of the time, it's caused by others' judgment or the actions of our caregivers, misinterpreted by our child-selves. Kids are totally self-absorbed, so anything their caregivers do is caused by the kid's behaviour. "Mommy is either ignoring me or hitting me because I'm a bad person." "Daddy is always yelling at me and doesn't love me because I'm unlovable."

Shame is put on us. And we have to do work to get rid of it. It's not our weight to carry, and it poisons our brain and our soul, and if we carry it too long, we go crazy. But the good news is resiliency enlarges our window, or moves it back down so the top is the top and the bottom is the bottom. And we can build our emotional resiliency up, with work.

16

ADDICTION

In which our hero describes being an addict, as addiction is often comorbid with mental illness.

So...let's talk about addiction.

Most of you know I don't drink because I'm an alcoholic. I'm also a real mean drunk. I don't like being an asshole.

In my journey to and through sobriety, I've learned some stuff.

Addicts don't use because we enjoy it.

We use to hide from our shit. We use so we don't have to face whatever it is we don't want to face. We use to numb the pain. To hide from ourselves.

Addiction is selfish. We put our need to hide before the people we love. Addicts can't get sober for someone, no matter how much they love that person. Which disgusts us, so we use.

Sobriety has to be selfish. An addict needs one thing they want more than they want to hide from themselves.

A lot of addicts just can't get sober on their own. We don't have the tools.

It's like repairing a car engine with a hacksaw and claw hammer. No matter how hard you work, all you're doing is wrecking shit.

An addict needs the right tools. Maybe that's AA, or a shrink, or religion, or SMART meetings, or rehab. Ideally, it's at least two of these.

Second-hardest thing I've ever done was get sober. Hardest thing is staying that way.

It's a daily fight. It gets easier, but it can sneak up on you.

Addicts obsess over yesterday; anything to make us feel bad so we can use.

Then we're disgusted for using. So we use to hide from that.

When addicts start trying to get clean, we obsess over tomorrow.

Today matters. Today I will not drink. Today I will do something to make a better tomorrow.

Nobody wants to be an addict.

It's a life of self-inflicted loneliness and pain.

Addicts push everyone away because we don't deserve to be loved.

Addicts tell ourselves they're leaving us because we don't deserve to be loved.

Addiction is a stone-cold bitch.

17

TO MY SONS #3

In which our hero makes a joke, reminding us to be good people for our own sake.

My sons, everybody needs a shot in the mouth once in a while.

I've been fortunate enough that every time I really needed a punch in the mouth, someone was around to provide it for me.

I try to pay that favour forward whenever I can.

There are worse things than getting punched in the mouth, and being an asshole is one of them.

If you're being an asshole, and someone lets you know with a shot in the yap, thank him later, when your mouth works properly again.

I love you.

18

LIFE OF AN ADDICT

In which our hero describes addiction further.

I was going to talk about grief today, but I can't. I'm too scared. So let's talk some more about addiction.

Those of you who've never battled addiction don't understand the totality of the shittiness.

An addict takes the pain we're causing others and internalizes it. We know we're hurting people who love us, and we hate ourselves for it.

There's nothing worse than that look.

The look in the face of the person you love most in all the world when you see them after you sober up. The look that says, "I love you, but right now you make me sick."

That look of disdain. That look cuts you to your soul.

That look hurts more than anything in the world possibly could.

No. I'm wrong. The other look hurts more.

The look of total helplessness in the face of the person you love more than anyone else in the world that says, "I see how much pain you're in; I love you so much; I know there's something very wrong; I don't know what it is; I don't know how to help you; I think it's my fault."

That look hurts worse than anything else ever could.

Because you know what's wrong.

It's the addiction. It's your need to hide from your shit. It's your fucking selfishness and cowardice and the knowledge you're ruining your life and the lives of everyone around you.

But it's easier and safer than facing whatever it is you're hiding from. So you use again to hide from the self-hate you feel for using again. And you hate yourself for doing that.

It's a shitty circle of hating yourself for hating yourself.

Recovery is a bullshit fairy-tale dream.

It's possible for others, maybe, but not for you.

Because nobody can hurt the way you're hurting.

You're all alone.

That's the life of an addict.

Self-loathing, and fear, and loneliness, and despair.

19

TO MY SONS #4

In which our hero outlines the Principles he learned to keep us mentally healthy.

To my sons, these are the Principles: Courage. Honesty. Responsibility. Perseverance.

Life is hard. We make it harder by lying, by quitting when it gets difficult, by shirking our duties, by not accepting challenges. Be brave. Be honest. We lie to ourselves, saying we're better or worse than we really are. The first is vanity disguising insecurity; the second is insecurity. Be honest with yourself, or you cannot be honest with anyone. Be honest or you'll stay dissatisfied and scared.

Honesty takes courage. Face fear. Fear of judgment, fear of failure, fear of fear. Responsibility takes courage in this age of victimhood and nation of cowards. Perseverance takes courage. Dare greatly and your failures will be many, but your successes will be heroic. Never quit. You can weep, vomit, bleed, sweat, swear, and ultimately not achieve the goal. But never quit and you cannot fail. Win or learn, never lose. Water wears away rock by persevering. "Be water, my friend," as Bruce Lee said.

Responsibility is the hallmark of an adult. Protect the weak; treat the ill; clothe the naked; house the homeless; care for the land. Do these things and you can walk with pride. The property I leave you was never mine, nor is it yours. The land of our ancestors belongs to your grandchildren's great-grandchildren.

Keep to the Rules. Guide your thoughts and deeds by the Principles, and you'll never suffer as I have from needless guilt, fear, shame, insecurity, loneliness, rage, desperation, and sorrow. Life will gift you enough of these things; don't create more for yourselves. I love you.

20

HELPING THE MENTALLY ILL

In which our hero explains how to best support the mentally ill.

Had an anxiety attack the other day, followed by a depressive episode. Came outta nowhere. My brain outsmarted me again, which, I'll admit, isn't difficult. But, c'mon…my brain knows exactly what I'm thinking, so outsmarting me in those circumstances is totally un-fucking-fair. Anyway, now that I got it back, here are some ideas about how to interact with somebody like me if you're somebody not like me.

1. Don't tell me to "get over it" or "move on." I mean, sure, it's great advice, very practical. But I've already thought of that. I did. Really. The Sheridan Dictionary definition of *clinical depression* is: the total inability to get over it and/or move on at the moment.

2. Likewise, if someone is having an anxiety attack, you're not being helpful in any way by saying "calm down" or "relax." The Sheridan Dictionary definition of *anxiety* is: the unique

capacity to not be able to calm down or relax because I don't fucking know why I'm not calm at the moment.

3. Don't suggest getting a drink. Giving a depressed person a depressant is unwise and ill-conceived. Blueberry pie and strong coffee won't cure depression, but they're fucking yummy, so get that instead.

Interacting with depression or anxiety or PTSD isn't infectious. You won't catch it by having coffee with me or hanging out with me for a bit once in a while. (Living with me, now that's contagious, and we'll discuss it in greater detail elsewhere.) I know trying to be my friend when I'm in an episode is tiring for you. I do. But it's way more tiring for me. When I'm like that, just putting my underwear on is as demanding on my body and mind as a ten-kilometre rucksack march. (Which is why I'm commando most of the time. Calm down, ladies; I'm taken.)

And trying to pretend I'm happy so you don't feel bad just makes me more tired, and I say and do stupid shit because my brain is at war with itself while I'm trying to talk with you and not let you know my brain is tearing itself apart. So I just go into grouchy old asshole mode and push everyone away because it's easier. Which is exactly the opposite of what my brain and soul need to recover. We need interaction and connection to be whole as humans. Other people like me go into withdrawal mode and hide from you for the same reasons.

Honestly, depression doesn't remove the need and want of people to connect and interact with other people, especially the ones we love. It removes our ability to do it. Understand, if I'm having an episode, you can talk to me about normal shit. I don't necessarily want to talk about the shit in my head. I want to hear how your kids are. What cool restaurant you went to. (Okay, maybe not with the current state of mass hysteria. Tell me about your toilet paper collection.)

You're not responsible for making me feel better. That isn't your job, and you don't have to try. Seriously. If I can't do it, you can't do it. You may worry you'll say the wrong thing or the conversation is gonna be weird and awkward. You won't, and it will anyway. That's okay. It's not you; it's me. You be you. That's it. That's your job. You can do it. I've got faith in you.

Depressed people can be depressed and still be okay. Our culture has an impossible obsession with happiness and tells us we should be happy 24/7 or we're messed up and broken. Not true.

Happiness is an instant, one second of awesome, not a steady state of being. I have a coffee with the perfect ratio of coffee to cream and sugar, boom, I'm happy. I drink it, it's gone; so is happy. Your depressed person can have fun with you by being involved in your life and doing things with or for you and be sad for themselves at the same time. We can do that. We're skilled multi-taskers that way.

Calling every day or texting every day is cool, but understand, we may not be physically or mentally able to respond right away. But that message, text, or voicemail is the best fucking thing we've had all goddamn day. We love you. We do. We just can't always say that to you. But we're always thinking it.

21

TO MY SONS #5

In which our hero encourages us, using fisticuffs as an allegory to fighting mental illness.

I'm a fighter, my sons. I was born a fighter, I've lived as a fighter, and I pursued careers that rewarded me for being a fighter. Being a fighter is why I've survived long enough to see your fifth and third birthdays. Because I fought poverty, neglect, addiction, depression, anxiety, PTSD, and suicidal ideation.

For me, and people like me, fighting isn't what we do; it's who we are. I'll always fight for love and for honour because that's what I am. I don't glorify violence, nor do I advocate violence for its own sake. But we must all fight sometimes.

You'll have to fight many times in your lives. Fight setbacks. Fight the desire to quit. Fight loneliness. Fight heartbreak. Fight sorrow. I talk about fighting here, but it has nothing to do with another human. I talk about the greater fight: the fight within you.

Don't try to be better than everyone around you. Try to be better than yourself every day. Try to make today's you better than yesterday's you, and tomorrow, do it again. Every day that goes by, I try to improve, searching for the impossible: perfection. I believe I'm capable of achieving the impossible.

I've achieved much thus far and will accomplish more. You may feel bad about losing, but you'll feel worse about underperforming, about not living up to your potential. If you don't perform to the best of your ability, it keeps you up at night and can cost you sleepless years of regret.

Nothing is given to you in this world, so work hard. To build mental toughness, you need to get comfortable with discomfort. Put yourself in the worst conditions you can, make yourself truly uncomfortable, and you can have a legitimate anticipation of succeeding, because you paid the price.

Show up. Today, do what others won't, so tomorrow, you can do what others can't. Know your strengths, but also know your weaknesses. Always work on your weaknesses; turn them into strengths.

You'll get tired, you'll get hurt, you'll hit adversity, and when you do, a lot of openings to quit will appear; find one reason to stay in the firefight. No one can hit you harder than life itself. How much can you suffer and keep fighting? How much punishment can you take and keep moving forward? That's how you win: perseverance. If you never quit fighting, you can always win. If you quit, you can never win.

Stupid people say, "Failure is not an option." Trust me, failure is always an option, and it's available at all times. But failure is a choice. You choose to fail or to succeed. If you learn from an experience, no matter whether you're declared the victor or not, then you've won. In all things, in all ways, you either win or you learn, and then you cannot lose. But failure is always an option, and it's important to accept that.

Fear of failure can spur you to victory, or it can freeze you in doubt. Never refuse to try because you're scared to fail. The greatest strength lies in rising each time we fail. Everybody starts out undefeated. The only people who stay undefeated are the ones who never fight. They're the same people who never achieve. I love you.

22

MENTAL ILLNESS IS CONTAGIOUS

In which our hero encourages us to look outside our own pain and work toward health and relationship.

I've talked (a lot) about mental illness. We haven't talked about it being contagious. People dealing with us for long periods of time when we're not stable...not good. Trying to deal with us when we're unpredictable, on a downslide, having an uncontrollable rage-filled tantrum...not good. Having to do that for years...super not good. Vicarious trauma is a real thing. So is caregiver fatigue. Look 'em up.

Having to deal with someone incapable of controlling their mood swings: imagine how exhausting that is. Babysitting a six-foot tall, 210-pound toddler? Nobody signs on for that. It's no wonder they resent, then hate, then despise us. How do they see us as adults after seeing us throw a tantrum? They're supposed to be our lovers and friends, not our nurses and nannies.

Walking on eggshells for years, never knowing what's going to set us off, but knowing something will. Trying to control every single aspect of existence to prevent the unpreventable, explosive anger...terrifying. And exhausting. Listening to our promises of change but no change. When do they stop believing? When do they stop listening? Then, when we get better, how do they believe it's real? How do they believe it's permanent, when it never has been before?

We get so deeply entrenched in that hole of pain and loneliness that we stop touching them, stop kissing or hugging them, stop interacting with them. Right when they need our support the most, we're incapable of providing it. But they push through. For as long as they can. Then they bail to save themselves, or they suffer their own trauma and burnout.

You know the signs. You know the symptoms. You lived them. Now look for them in that person who's been trying to support you all this time. Look for the grief, depression, anxiety, irritability, anger...you know them. Look for the isolating behaviour, alcohol or drug dependency, inability to focus, memory loss, sleep loss, overeating or not eating, or avoidance behaviour. Look for that hopelessness you felt, that disconnection from humanity, that loss of purpose. Look for that permanent exhaustion. Ask yourself if they still seem to want to be with you or if they seem to hate you now?

Listen to them; make sure they still feel worthy of love. Because they are. You fucking owe them that.

23

TO MY SONS #6

In which our hero encourages us to fight insecurity and let go of regret.

Fighting is life, and life is a fight, my sons. (Hopefully I haven't screwed up so badly you're literally fighting for survival. But it's an excellent analogy, comparing fighting to life itself.) You both fought to exist, from your moments of conception. Every day, something is trying to kill you for its own existence, even if that is a virus, a germ, or a bacterium. The law of the jungle is unbreakable and enforced everywhere. My fiercest fights have been with myself, the battlefield my own brain. That's why I fear no external battle.

To keep battling and overcome obstacles in the face of overwhelming odds is what makes a fighter. You can do everything perfectly and still fail, but that's no excuse to quit. Try, fall, get up, try again, fall, get up, try again. That's life: a never-ending struggle to not die, while steadily proceeding to death. So you can either exist until you die, or you can live and struggle to be better than you were yesterday, struggle to make life better for the following generations.

A black belt is a white belt who didn't quit. A champion is a contender who fought past failure. One workout won't change you, but a dozen will. Perseverance and consistency in training. Time plus effort equals success. Progress only comes in small increments. Patience, diligence, and consistency is the path to continual improvement.

It's a never-ending grind to try to make yourself the best person you can be. There'll be many situations where you can either rise to meet adversity or quit and feel sorry for yourself. That's going to be your decision. Imagine meeting the person you could've been if you hadn't quit. Now work to make that man a reality. Be that man by never quitting.

Some fear to try and settle for mediocrity. They fear to set their goals too high, lest they never meet them. The danger lies not in setting your goal high and failing to reach it, but in setting your goal too low and reaching it. Nothing important in life is easy. Nothing easy is important. Work hard. It takes failure to achieve success, just as it takes being afraid to be courageous.

I know this to be true, for I was weak and cowardly. That insecurity kept me from pursuing my lifelong dream of becoming a commando. Once I overcame that fear, my life became what I'd always wanted it to be. Mediocrity isn't failing. Mediocrity is not trying. Fear of failure is the same thing as fear of success; both are fear of trying. Avoid mediocrity by trying, whether you fail utterly or triumph heroically. Never fear to fail; fear not trying.

Every time you take a beatdown and rise up again, you rise up stronger and wiser. Wisdom is the result of taking an ass-whooping. And nobody will hand you an ass-whooping like life itself. Wisdom comes from failure; failure comes from trying. Just as you cannot be brave unless first you're scared, so you cannot become wise until you fail.

Bravery and wisdom are habits. The habit of never quitting. Embrace the suck. Take shit and take point.

One of the keys to wisdom for me has been to let go of the mistakes, the regrets, the shame of the past. It's important to remember the past, but you mustn't torture yourself by reliving every regret every day, gnawing your pain and shame in the darkness of your soul, like a dog with a bone.

I've made many mistakes, but regret builds character and makes us better people, if we use it as the tool it's meant to be. Learn from your guilt and regret to ensure you never make that mistake again, then (and this is the hard part for me), then...let it go. Holding regret is like holding a burning ember in your fist to throw at an enemy. Keeping shame in your soul is like eating poison berries to fill your belly. I love you.

24

THOUGHTS ON THE DEPRESSED BRAIN

In which our hero summarizes points made earlier, following a massive anxiety attack that caused him to start all fucking over again. It happens, dear reader. Never quit. It's worth it.

If we don't tell our brain what to do, it'll do what it wants.

If that brain has had certain or several negative experiences, what it wants to do isn't good for it.

Like a kid. Wants to eat only candy.

Not good for it. But it'll do anything to get that candy.

If we don't realize and accept the problem is internal, and keep blaming external factors, we don't deal with our shit.

So we don't heal.

Doesn't matter where we go, or for how long, or who with, the problem is us, and it comes along.

Doesn't matter what substance we use, we sober up, and we're still there. So's our shit. Plus a headache.

The depressed brain wants to isolate but needs connection. Tell the brain what to do.

Name the monster. We can't fight something we don't accept is real. We name it, we tame it.

Our shit is our shit. It's our perception and reaction to nouns: to people, places, things, events. It's not the noun. It's us.

Get the tools. Can't fix a Chevy small-block with a hacksaw and claw hammer. Just makes a bigger mess. Go to a mechanic; get advice; get a socket set.

Now we can fix some shit.

Can't do it alone. That's how we get worse.

The cure for depression, anxiety, PTSD, addiction: connection.

Grow your circle. Fill it with the right people. People who are or have been fighting that monster.

Tell the brain what to do. Or it'll do what it wants.

Use the conscious mind to understand what the unconscious and subconscious minds are doing.

Get tools.

Get guidance.

Get to work.

You're not alone.

You matter.

25

CHANGE YOUR WORLD

In which our hero talks about the negative perception illness causes us to see everywhere.

I've been hearing this sort of thing a lot the past couple days: "I hope this year is better than last year," or "Hopefully, 2021 is better than 2020."

Dude, what are you doing to make it better? Hope all you want.

Deeds, not wishes, accomplish things. You want 2021 to be better? Make it better.

The world is a steaming bilious cesspit filled with evil and sorrow and pain.

Unless you don't want it to be. If everything is awful, everywhere you go, with everyone you know, there's one common denominator.

Change the world by changing your perception of it. Perception is reality. The world is how we see it.

When we're dark, we see the world dark.

If we work hard at not seeing it that way, we stop seeing it that way, and it stops being that way.

Change the way you see the world, you change the world.

It's all in your perspective: Are you trapped in the darkness? Or are you walking toward the light?

Help yourself by helping someone else. Make your life a little less like a living hell by making someone else's life a little bit less hellish. It works.

Be kind. Find the strength to be open and compassionate with others, and it starts to work on you too. You start being kind to yourself, and the world stops being a giant ball of shit.

Depression starts to lose its grip on you; same with anxiety, same with PTSD, same with addiction.

You deserve it, you know.

You deserve kindness. From others, sure, but mostly from you.

You matter. If not to yourself, you matter to me. So, if you can't be kind to you for you, do it for me.

I know, 2020 sucked; 2021 doesn't have to.

Don't let it.

You don't have to live in the dark forever.

I chose not to. You can too.

It ain't ever easy, but it gets easier all the time.

It's totally worth the work, I promise.

26

TO MY SONS #7

In which our hero allegorically connects poverty to mental illness and the struggle for fiscal stability to that of mental stability.

For most of my life, I've either had little money or spent money foolishly because I lived for instant gratification. A common occurrence amongst the poorer classes. It's why poor kids wear gold chains and $300 sneakers but can't afford car payments and their babies live on Doritos.

Poor kids like me don't learn about tax-free saving accounts and investments and delayed gratification. It's difficult to see far enough into the future to picture the result of investing when you're focused on surviving the moment. When you can't imagine a future, you don't bother with putting money aside, or even conceive of a reason to do so.

Now I earn good money and I picture every obstacle like it's a man trying to take what's mine and send me back to poverty and aimless existence. That obstacle has to be overcome for your sake. I fight the economy and my own desires for possessions I don't need in order to win the war by ensuring you never suffer financially.

If you truly believe in yourself, enhance your knowledge and skills, and never stop trying. Most times, it's enough to succeed. Incorporate guts, courage, will, and wit because talent is never enough. Talent alone is unsustainable. Talent has an end; passion fades. Effort never ends. Belief builds on itself. Persistence is sustainable. Intelligence grows. I had raw athletic talent and an extraordinary intellect. And I wasted it because I never learned to work hard, focus, and embrace the suck. I relied on talent, and eventually, it wasn't enough anymore. This is a case, my sons, of do as I fucking say and not as I did.

You're never so good you can't get better. That's the champion's mentality. A champion practises the basics a thousand times a day, every day. Everything is built on the basics. Take that mentality and apply that to everything in your life. The key to success in life is to set goals, then go after those goals, and don't hold anything back.

Success or failure, effort is its own reward. If you try your hardest and know you could do no better, then failure is just a setback, and you'll feel no shame or regret. Be better than yesterday. Tomorrow, do it again. No matter how dark things are today, tomorrow morning the sun is going to rise.

You win a fight, you rarely learn from it. You lose a fight and survive, you better learn from it. Losing sucks, but in losing you learn the most. You may fall, but you must always get up because champions are crowned on their feet, not their knees. You may get knocked down, but you must always get back up.

He may beat you today, but when he has to face you again, and again, and again, either you'll beat him or he'll leave town to get the hell away from you.

Loss is a part of life; if you don't lose, you don't grow. If it doesn't test you, it doesn't change you. Everything important in life is simple and never easy. Everything important in life is difficult. That's what makes it worthwhile. This isn't tough-love advice; this is life. You don't quit when you get beat; you pick yourself up and start working to achieve your goals. If you keep pursuing your goals with single-minded devotion and unceasing effort, eventually you'll make good things happen. Everyone encounters adversity; it's how you come back from it that defines the human you are. I love you.

27

CHANGE YOUR PERSPECTIVE

In which our hero explains how to change a negative viewpoint to combat depression.

I've talked about changing your perspective. Here's an example: I was such a shitty father, I needed to kill myself.

I needed to make sure my son wouldn't end up like me because I'm such a shitty person.

I had to die.

It was the only logical option.

Eventually I was able to ask my crazy, "Exactly how am I the worst father in the world." It had no answer.

So I reminded my crazy I never sexually or physically abused him. Therefore, I'm not the worst father in the world. I pointed out he's fed, clothed, and has a roof over his head because I go to a job I despise with every fibre of my being.

Then I reminded my crazy I read parenting books so I'd be a good parent. By definition, therefore, because I try to be a good dad, I'm a good dad.

If I don't try, I'm a shitty dad. Shitty people don't care they're shitty. That's why they're shitty.

Wasn't easy. But it's simple.

Everything that matters is simple and rarely easy. Big difference.

Running a marathon is simple: don't stop running. It ain't easy.

I explained it to inmates I used to counsel like this: imagine your brain is a beach. Water flows down to the sand, finds a low spot, builds up, finds another, all the way to the ocean. Eventually, it's the St. Lawrence Seaway.

Yeah? With me?

Same thing with our thoughts.

We get trapped in a way of thinking, and everything sucks because we suck.

That's the thought pattern our illness dictates, whether it be trauma or a quirk in our DNA. (Or both. Hello, my name is Sheridan and I have wonky brain chemistry and trauma.) So every thought we have flows down the same pathway in our brain and makes that pathway deeper and wider because it's used the most.

So we get trapped in hell.

Here's the thing: it's fucking sand!

Ya gotta learn to recognize those thoughts and stop 'em.

At first, you won't catch 'em until you're way the fuck out in a riptide, past Iceland.

But you caught it. And you'll catch it faster every time.

Eventually, ya catch 'em at the beach, start digging a new trench, and backfill the old one.

I kept reminding my crazy about how trying meant I was a good dad.

New canal dug.

Two years later, it's not easy. But it's simple.

My brain still tries to go back to old thought patterns sometimes.

But I catch it faster and easier all the time.

You can too.

Professional help is pretty damn important here.

You want to dig a new canal, you need an engineer, y'know?

I did it. You can too.

Grab a shovel.

28

SIMPLE, NOT EASY

In which our hero uses his experience to illustrate the above point.

So...change perspective, and tell your brain what to do. What the Kentucky-fried fuck do I mean by that? Lemme explain it as I understand it. (Gonna be some swearing, maybe some crying. Put on your big boy/girl panties; some of this still hurts a lot.)

Okay...when my son was born, I totally snapped. I'd been teetering on the edge for a couple years before...fuck...before she died. Then, when it happened, I went apeshit crazy. The plan was to find the dogs a home and then find a war somewhere and kill until I died. Failing that, just whack myself.

Then Dennette came along and exploded into and took over my life, thereby saving it. (Whoooo, anxiety sweat is dripping off me right now. This vulnerability shit is scary and hard. You assholes better appreciate it.)

Fast-forward months, maybe a bit over a year, I'm not sure.

Anyway, my son is booties on the ground. And I have no control over my brain at fucking all! I don't end it because, despite needing to kill myself to save my family from my influence, there's this tiny voice saying things like "studies show children without a father do more poorly in life" and "if you use a firearm to kill yourself, the RCMP will use that to further inflate their false 'gun-crime' statistics."

I get help.

Fast-forward again, three years. I'm stable. I experience moments of peace and joy.

What'd I do? I changed my perspective.

That helped me tell my brain what to do.

Because up 'til then, part of my brain was driving the bus. The amygdala and the hypothalamus, specifically.

Really useful for scary situations like combat or a bear stalking you.

Utterly fucking counterproductive for being a dad or husband.

Children do what we do, not what we say they should do. A leader models the behaviour they want their subordinates to exhibit.

So, not wanting my son to be like me, because I'm the biggest piece of shit on the planet, I start trying to act like the man I want my son to become.

Eventually, I became the man I want my sons to be. I'm good if they turn out like this version of me.

Fake that shit. Fake it until you fucking make it.

Change the course of the river. Dig a new canal and backfill the old riverbed.

Decide who you want to be, and fucking pretend to be that person!

It's that simple. And it's really, really fucking hard.

Everything in life that matters is simple, and never easy.

29

THIRTY-SIX-HOUR FLASHBACK

In which our hero relates a flashback to remind us our brain is physically different than it once was.

Not cool.

Funny, I know everything about PTSD.

Completely forgot flashbacks can last days sometimes.

Total sympathetic nervous system activation.

Tunnel vision, auditory exclusion.

The whole bit.

Amygdala hijack.

Couldn't get the rest of the brain involved to save my life.

Literally.

Brain of a person with PTSD, depression, anxiety, is physically and chemically different.

It's injury, but the injury isn't visible.

There's no scar.

Gotta remember that.

So do you, if you're like me, or love someone like me.

30

TO MY SONS #8

In which our hero introduces the idea of grace, tying it to gratitude, continuing positive psychology.

Grateful, graceful, and great, my sons. Gratitude: being thankful; showing appreciation for and returning kindness. Grace: disposition to or an act or instance of kindness, courtesy, or clemency; quality of being pleasantly polite; or a willingness to be fair and honest. Gratitude keeps you humble when things go well and keeps you from resentment when they don't. Grace in victory and defeat displays character others will respect and admire, causing you to maintain self-respect and stay honourable.

When things are going well, strive for gratitude; when things are going badly, strive for grace. Greatness is a lifelong mission, requiring constant vigilance against baser instincts and darker thoughts. Stick to the Rules, follow the Principles, stay grateful, stay graceful, and greatness will be yours.

If you want something to be, it's up to you to will it into existence. You must create it with thought and deed and will, whether that be a tangible object or a set of circumstances. Belief is a powerful thing. I don't speak of religious or spiritual belief, but self-belief. For he who believes in himself, anything's possible. Believe in yourself, never quit, and find purpose. A man with purpose, self-belief, and who won't quit is a man who cannot be denied.

A man who has never fallen has never stood for something. I've been jokingly referred to as a legend. I'm not, just a man who never quit. I pushed my body and mind to breaking, then rebuilt them. I haven't quit because I have purpose: you.

Some people concern themselves with comfort. Until you step out of comfort, life doesn't begin. Comfort is stagnation, and stagnation is decay. Comfort isn't living; it's existing. Sheep exist. If you're not chasing dreams, you're existing. Don't exist; live. I existed for years before I followed my dream of being a commando and began to live.

None of us are promised tomorrow. When opportunity presents itself to you, take it. There are two things you must do in life: die, and live until you die. What happens in between is up to you. You can exist comfortably, or you can live.

Seek to be comfortable in discomfort. Strive. Fail. Strive. Will, like the body, must be trained. Ceaselessly seeking discomfort, resisting comfort, this is how you train your will. Embrace the suck, and walk the warrior's path. Walking the warrior's path isn't about being better than someone else; it's about striving to be the best you that you can be, and about bringing out the best in others around you.

I've learned when I'm afraid of something not to avoid it. Fear ruled my life for years. To overcome fear, you must first face it, then embrace it. Only then can you let it go. Courage isn't the absence of fear. Courage is doing what you must despite fear.

The greatest fear is the fear of losing, for that's the fear of trying. Don't waste time and effort thinking about losing and failure; just do it.

If you let fear stop you from fulfilling your dreams, you rob yourself of more than dreams. You rob yourself of pride. Not starting because you're scared to fail is the worst form of quitting and will cause you the deepest regret. Die with memories, not regrets.

Your mother is my hero because life is about overcoming adversity, and I watched her overcome so much adversity in our life together but still smile the smile that takes away my breath, draws tears from my eyes, and stops my heart. It's one thing to overcome adversity but be bitter and angry and carry pain or sorrow forever; that has been me until very recently. Your mother overcame adversity and still smiles. That's strength.

I've cried much and smiled seldom for most of my life. Anger, resentment, regret, shame, rage, guilt...these things have taken most of my years until late. Until your mother and you. Trust me, smiling is better. Your mother taught me that. Heed her lesson. I love you.

31

YOU DON'T FIGHT ALONE

In which our hero reminds us we are not alone, despite the depressed mind's beliefs.

No matter how dark things get, no matter how alone you feel, never stop fighting.

I've walked through those shadows.

I'll walk through that darkness again, with you.

I've fought those demons before.

I'll fight them again, with you.

You have value.

You have worth.

You're loved.

No matter what, never stop fighting.

I will fight beside you.

You're not alone.

Reach out.

32

KINTSUGI

In which our hero equates pottery to brains, illustrating mental illness doesn't "ruin" us.

I broke. Sure did.

And I got no problem saying it.

Now.

We have this idea we need to hide our pain and scars.

Fucking stigma bullshit.

My pain is what happened to me, and it's how I know where to put the effort into healing. (Healing: noun, the process of making or becoming sound or healthy again.)

My scars are my trophies.

We have this idea damage is only repaired if it's done so completely there's no sign of the damage at all.

We have to hide damage.

Everything has to be perfect.

Except nothing's perfect.

Ever.

Anywhere.

Applying the same mentality to healing our brains is counterproductive.

We're never going to be like someone who hasn't dealt with our shit.

Doesn't mean they're better.

Doesn't mean they're worse.

Means they're people.

Trying to erase our shit completely and make our brains perfect is…well, it's stupid.

And it makes us worse because we try to create something that can't exist.

So we shit on ourselves for "failing" and start that downward spiral and holyshitherewegoagainmakeitstopmakeitstop makeitstop!

Kintsugi: Japanese art of repairing broken pottery by mending the breakage with lacquer mixed with powdered precious metal.

The cracks and breaks are made immediately visible.

Unbroken cups all look the same, but that one, now.

The breaks are stronger, beautiful, and forever.

Like the ones in my brain.

I won't ever be good as new.

I'm making myself stronger and more uniquely beautiful every day.

The healed breaks are the signs of my struggles, my healing, my resiliency, and my success.

The beautiful scars display the hurt I recovered from, show me I'm whole and I got here through effort and pain and breakage.

I ain't good as new.

I ain't perfect.

I'm better.

Knights in shining armour have never had their armour tested.

Mine's rebuilt to withstand stronger blows than I've received.

Kintsugi: show off your scars.

They're beautiful.

Be proud.

You're a survivor.

33

TO MY SONS #9

In which our hero introduces the idea of discipline being necessary to defeat the chaos of mental illness, allegorically connecting it to being a warrior.

My sons, to live life fully, multiply all the facets of your life and learn to see from perspectives other than your first one. Keep yourself open to new ideas, and try new things. If it should turn out you don't like the experience, take pride in knowing you've worked to become a more well-rounded human being. Strive to be a true Renaissance man. Leonardo da Vinci was a painter, engineer, scientist, soldier, theorist, sculptor, and architect who could bend horseshoes in his bare hands and bought caged birds to set them free.

Learn constantly. Learn from everyone. Study everything. Curiosity is your greatest teacher; choose to follow it. Nothing in the universe is separate from anything else; all things are connected, so your studies should be too. Mediocrity is stagnation. Growth is life. Choose to grow in any and every direction that strikes your fancy.

Let no man wrong those under your protection with impunity. Fighting out of vanity is the height of stupidity. Fight for honour; fight for love; fight for those who cannot fight. Fools say violence never solves anything. Actually, violence solves many things, but if used by the wrong people, the solution is to the detriment of humanity. Violence is seldom the answer, but when it is, it's the only answer.

Following the warrior's path has taken me to places I was afraid to go. But always, when I got there, I was glad I made the journey. You never know yourself until you're at your weakest. True strength isn't measured in how much weight you can lift. It's measured in persevering. True strength is found in constantly testing yourself, never becoming complacent, always pushing yourself in all ways.

You get stronger and faster by training on the days you don't want to. You grow tougher by overcoming laziness and pushing through exhaustion or boredom. It may not be a great workout, but you've overcome weakness. You've exercised your will, if not your body, and the will is far more important. You've embraced the suck and taken another step along the warrior's path. Training, really, is just being comfortable with being uncomfortable.

Discipline allows us to be uncomfortable. Discipline grants us consistency, and consistency is growth. Discipline grants us perseverance. Champions are champions because they work past exhaustion when no one is watching.

Knowledge of self-defence grants us self-confidence. Self-confidence grants us self-control. Self-control banishes fear. Fear's the enemy. Fear's what we must learn to defeat. Everybody knows fear. The difference is the coward doesn't control fear, and the brave does. Fear doesn't stop death; it stops life.

No matter what you do or don't do in this life, you'll die someday, so until that day, live your life to its fullest. Dare greatly, laugh loudly, love hard, accept the pain and sorrow that'll come, and then do it all again. It's only pain, it cannot hurt you unless you let it, and scars are reminders of memories. The scars on my body, my mind, and my soul are reminders of how I became the man I am today. I love you.

34

WE'RE NOT ALONE

In which our hero relates facts about mental illness and reiterates we are not alone.

Several months ago, I was talking with my neighbours, and one of them said something that has resonated ever since: "Your brain is unreliable." That shook my entire reality. And she said it so calmly, too, so matter-of-factly.

So simple. Not easy. But true, and that's why it sticks. If you're like me, your brain's unreliable too. It lies to you all the god-damn time about everything.

How do you know when it's lying? Well, if it's saying really horrible things about you, straight to you...it's lying. We don't say horrible things to people's faces. If your brain's saying things to you that you'd never say to another human, it's lying.

The second way to know your brain's lying is when it tries to tell you that you're all alone. That nobody cares. That you're unworthy of love. That you're the only person who feels this way. That there's something fundamentally wrong with you. That you're so shitty, you deserve to be lonely.

Lies. Bollocks. Poppycock. Stuff and nonsense. Straight-up bullshit. Would you say that shit to someone else? Then why are you saying it to you? Stop being so mean to yourself. Life doesn't need your help; it'll be mean enough to you all by itself. Sturgill Simpson is right: life ain't fair and the world is mean. Here's a dozen fun little facts about mental illness.

- **Fun Fact 1:** Mental illness hits every single family in Canada at some point. Ya catch that shit? Every single Canadian is going to be affected by mental illness, even if they don't suffer from it themselves. It might be a family member, a friend, a lover, or a co-worker, but e'rbody in Canada is gonna hafta take a bite out of this shit sandwich.
- **Fun Fact 2:** Mental illness can strike anybody. It's not a character flaw, a lack of willpower, or any of that bullshit. It's caused by a complicated mix of heredity, personality, and experience. Some of it's genetic; some of it's environmental; it's nature and nurture. Shitty things can happen, maybe one giant awful thing or maybe a whole lifetime of smaller awful things, that overwhelm our ability to cope because we didn't learn healthy coping mechanisms. Or we just get dealt a bad hand at conception and hafta learn to play it, like my serotonin deficiency or post-partum depression (which can affect fathers too. Dudes, you also have hormonal fluctuations throughout the month. You get your period too. She's not the only crazy one in the house that week. Own your shit).
- **Fun Fact 3:** One out of every five people in this country is personally facing some kind of mental health trouble or

straight-up illness. Look around; if there's five of you in the room, one of you's hurting. If it ain't you, someone in the room is battling for their life. So be kind. They could use an ally.

- **Fun Fact 4:** The way things are going, if we don't fix some shit...raise our babies to be more emotionally resilient... stop all this cancel-culture bullshit...stop blaming others for our shit...start trying to be more open and curious with each other...start trying connection and compassion...stop with the social media garbage and start living in this reality together...stop staying awake later than we should and turn off the screens a half hour before bed...start exercising regularly and eating sensibly...well, fuck...before they get out of their thirties, around half—half!!—of Canadians will be suffering through, or recovering from, a mental illness of some kind. So can we please all just agree to stop screwing up our babies? They're not snowflakes, nor are they the enemy.

- **Fun Fact 5:** Mental illness can hit anybody regardless of age, education, income level, and cultural background. I don't like R.E.M.'s music, but they got it right: everybody hurts. Now, the lower your education and/or income level, the higher the likelihood you may face some kind of mental health trouble or straight-up illness. Certain cultural backgrounds also exponentially increase those odds. For instance, if you're Indigenous or the child of immigrants from certain parts of the world, including many parts of Africa versus Europe.

- **Fun Fact 6:** Approximately 5 to 10 percent of Canadian adults will experience clinical depression at some time in their lives. I think the last stat I saw on an official Canadian government website said 8 percent. With 37,742,154 Canadians...8 percent is...what? Three million? We aren't alone.

- **Fun Fact 7:** Approximately 5 percent of Canadians will struggle with an anxiety disorder, so that's...something near two million, right? Anxiety is a straight-up bitch, and I'll tell the world for nuthin'. Some days, I'm mildly off; some days I'm so fucked up I can't function.
- **Fun Fact 8:** Close to one-half of the people who say they feel like they're struggling with depression or anxiety have never gone to a doctor about it. They may go to a doctor for some of the symptoms, like low energy, but they haven't been able to talk to a medical professional about their mental health problem. So they suffer alone and die alone, too often by their own hand. Screw stigma: speak out, reach out.
- **Fun Fact 9:** The real problem isn't the mental illness. It's the fucking stigma we haven't gotten rid of. It's the fear of judgment! It's fear. It's judgment. We're killing our friends and family because of stigma. People aren't getting help because they're scared of what we might say about them. The biggest problem with mental illness is it drives isolation. The cure is connection. The cure to fear is knowledge; fear comes from ignorance. Educate yourself, then educate those you care about. One of them is fighting for their life and is too scared of judgment to let you help them. For fuck's sake, talk about it. My wife died alone in her own head and in pain because she couldn't talk about it. I miss her every day, I regret almost every day of our last two years together, and I carry endless shame. Mental illness is the loneliest place in the world. Fuck, I wish you could see the tears on my face. Maybe it'd help you find the courage to say, "Screw stigma."
- **Fun Fact 10:** Mental illnesses can be treated with therapy and sometimes meds. I know this to be true. I've done it and am doing it. Nobody has to live that way. Nobody has to

die that way. If you can find the strength to ask for the help, it's there and it works. If you aren't suffering, talking about mental illness in a non-judgmental and compassionate way around people may be exactly what a sufferer needs to hear to get the help they need. It's an illness, and illnesses can be treated and recovered from.

- **Fun Fact 11:** You're loved. Here's how I know: every one of you has someone you love so much, you'd die for them. If you love someone that much, they love you back the same amount. That's how that shit works. You know it's true.
- **Fun Fact 12:** If you're in a place so dark you can't believe anybody else is there for you, understand: I am.

35

60/40

In which our hero relays relationship advice, as connection is vital to mental health.

When I first was getting married, the padre told us relationships aren't 50/50, they're 60/40.

If both of you give 50 percent, there's a boundary, a line where you'll butt heads.

Each of you will think you're giving more than the other and become resentful.

He said you each have to give 60 percent and expect 40 percent back.

That gives you a buffer zone of 20 percent each.

He was right.

But not 100 percent right.

Sometimes it's 80/20 because your partner's really struggling that day.

I don't know how many 80 percent days Dennette has in her, but I'm eternally grateful she keeps finding them.

I don't know how many 80 percent days I have in me, but I'm gonna keep trying to find them.

Meanwhile, I'm pretty glad for that regular 20 percent.

36

TO MY SONS #10

In which our hero reminds us of the importance of love, gratitude, and perseverance to mental health.

My sons, if you don't love yourself, who'll do it for you? I spent my life hating myself. It was a lesson I learned in childhood: I'm without worth as a person and therefore unlovable. Despite that, two women loved me greatly. And I did my level best to ruin it.

My inability to overcome my insecurity, my fear of them seeing the real me kept me insane, trying to push them away while desperately hoping they wouldn't leave. That's insanity, and I was insane. My first wife died in part because insanity drove a wedge between us that neither of us had the strength to push aside.

Love yourselves because you have intrinsic worth and value beyond measure and are deserving of love. Love yourselves first, and then you'll be able to love others as they deserve to be loved. Love's a powerful weapon in this fight.

Gratitude's as important a weapon in your fight as love. One's a shield; the other's a sword. Gratitude will protect you from most negative emotions, like resentment and depression. It's hard to be negative when you're grateful. It's hard to feel like a victim when you're focusing on the things in your life you're thankful for. If you feel like you've nothing to be happy about today, be grateful there will be a tomorrow, with all of its potential. Look around and you'll find something to be grateful for, even if it's just that today, with all its shittiness, will eventually be over.

Learn from yesterday, put those lessons into play today, and you can make tomorrow better. But remember, you're living today. You can't live yesterday or tomorrow. One's gone; the other doesn't exist yet. You're living today. So live today.

A journey of a thousand miles begins with a single step. And it continues one step at a time. Look back to see how far you've come, look ahead to see how much closer your goal is, but remember to keep stepping, one at a time. Make each step count. And stop once in a while to just enjoy the view. It's a journey, after all. It'll end eventually, and you may never see those sights again. Take advantage of today. It's pretty special.

Five years ago (my sons, today as I write this, you're five and three; I don't know how old you are now, reading this), I came to a place in my life where I was hopeless. I had to kill myself to save you from becoming me, because I wished that on nobody, especially not the most precious, most dear, most important thing I'd ever encountered: you, my son. And if I'd killed myself, my incredible younger son, my lovely little terror, you wouldn't have existed, and that would've been a crime against the universe. My only hope was to change everything or die. Fight or quit. So I fought.

I fought my brain, and I do it daily. As long as you fight, you cannot lose. If you never quit, it's just another round. You can always make up that round and score a submission or a KO. If you leave everything in the ring, in the cage, on the mat, it doesn't matter if you win or not; you can never lose.

It's about embracing the grind, always being willing to get back up when you're knocked down. Take the eight-count if you must, but get up before ten. Put in the hours of roadwork, of countless reps, of getting tapped out over and over. Work hard. Sweat in training so you don't bleed in battle. And when shit's going bad, when life's shit-kicking you square in the junk repeatedly, it's about not getting down on yourself and just getting up and getting back to work.

Strive. Be the best you that you can be. I love you.

37

GUY FALLS IN A HOLE

In which our hero relays a parable. Or an allegory. Or something.

Guy falls in a hole. Too deep to jump it. Sides keep collapsing; can't climb out.

Random dude walks by; guy calls for help. Dude throws him some money; tells him to buy a ladder.

Guy's like, what the fuck?

Another dude walks by. Guy says, "Help! I can't get out!" Dude's a doctor. Gives him a prescription; says, "Here, you'll feel better." Leaves.

Guy's still in the hole.

Another dude walks by. Hears the guy; asks, "How did you get here? Were you born there? Did your parents put you there?" Guy talks for an hour. Dude's a psychologist; says he'll be back next week.

Guy's freaking out. He's gonna die in a fuckin' hole because nobody's helping him.

Another dude walks by. "Help!" Dude's a priest and says, "Let's pray." Kneels down. Prays. Says, "Trust in God." Leaves.

Guy gives up, lies down in the bottom of the hole, and waits to die, exhausted, scared, and lonely.

Another dude stops; asks, "You stuck?" Guy says, "Yeah. Nobody'll help me. I don't care anymore. I'll die in this hole." Dude jumps in the hole with him. Guy goes, "What the fuck? Now we'll both die!" Dude says, "It's okay. I've been here before. I know how to get out."

First heard this story in jail. Decide for yourself which side of the bars I was on.

The hole can be addiction or mental illness.

I've been in both, and I know the way out.

I'll jump back in.

(I've decided: it's a fable. I've had so much help from random strangers, my doctor, several psychologists, and a priest.)

38

MENTORSHIP

In which our hero reminds us we're fallible but can always learn and improve.

Y'know, I'm regarded as an excellent mentor and teacher.

It's not because I know a lot of shit. I don't.

It's not because I'm highly professional. I'm not.

It's not because I'm always right. I'm not.

It's because I've spent soooo much time being wrong.

Trust me, I know what it looks like when you're about to screw up.

I already did it at least once.

39

TO MY SONS #11

In which our hero reiterates the importance of gratitude, fortitude, and self-esteem to prevent mental illness.

My sons, I'm an alcoholic. (You may already know that. I don't know how old you are now, reading this.) I pray neither of you inherited the genes to give you the predilection to addictive behaviour, and your grandparents, mother, and I've given you the emotional tools so you never feel the need to hide from your problems with a chemical, be it booze, weed, or something truly shitty. Remember this: addiction isn't the problem. It's a failed mechanism used to cope with the problem. No matter how drunk or high you may get, the problem is still going to be there when you sober up or come down. And now you still have the same problem, and you feel like hammered dog shit.

Smart isn't wise. They aren't the same thing. (You're so terribly, frighteningly smart. It's scary how smart you are, both in your own way.) Wise can be reached from smart, but there are no shortcuts to it. The advice I give you is designed to make your life easier, based on the wisdom I've gained, but you'll have to make your own mistakes to gain wisdom. Even if that wisdom is just "Well, fuck. The old man was right."

If you've wronged another, apologize, and mean it. You'll both be better for it. If you've done nothing wrong, don't apologize. Don't compromise your morals or your honour for the sake of conformity.

Don't compare yourself to other people around you. The only person you must surpass is you from yesterday. Compare yourself to that person. You aren't in competition with anyone else in the battle of life. You're competing with you. To become who you want to be, you must be willing to let go of unnecessary parts of yourself.

Travel light. You don't need most of the baggage you might have. Life's gonna fuck with you. Don't take it personally. That way lies depression and anxiety. Life fucks everyone over; it ain't personal. It's an opportunity to get better.

Humility and confidence aren't antonyms. They walk hand in hand. You can have both at once. Humility will come from the world. Confidence must come from you. Project confidence, not arrogance. Be humble, not ashamed.

Everyone's a tough guy until an actual tough guy walks by. Everyone wants to be seen as a badass, but very few want to do what badasses must do in order to be a badass. When you can push through fear and pain, fear and pain are no longer factors to be considered. It'll be impossible to have your will broken. Embrace the suck. Make yourself mentally stronger. Do things to make your body and mind scream at you to quit, then…don't.

I won't quit. I won't break, and I'll fight like a dog, tooth and nail, every day for you. This is my promise to you, my boys.

Take nothing for granted, not a day, not a minute, not a person. Cherish them. Days, minutes, and people pass. Die with memories, not wishes. Tell the people you love that you love them while they live. Apologize to those you've wronged today. Hold no grudges. Settle accounts now. I love you.

40

GRIEF #1

In which our hero relays his experience with grief.

Some terrible coincidences have led me to write about grief in hopes it helps somebody.

Grief, temporarily, made my ordinarily fragmented mind whole. Like a burning hot glue, it cemented all the normally shifting, shattered pieces of my mind in place. It was as though the pain put my brain back together. You see, grief wasn't inside me. The poets get that all wrong. My small, frail body couldn't contain the universality, the completeness, of my grief. Pain was ripping my soul apart. Pain was tearing my heart to pieces. Pain was everything. Pain was everywhere. The totality of the pain held me together as a being composed of pain. Grief, pain, wasn't inside my body. Not only inside my body, anyway.

No, grief surrounded me and flowed through me like freezing water, as it permeated every fibre and molecule and atom of my being and enveloped me in a cloud of stifling darkness that kept me from seeing or hearing the world. I'd been in pain for years, but now I was pain. Everything was pain. The universality of my grief drove me even further into isolation, buoying me afloat while its immensity was pushing me under. It comforted me with its familiar but new loneliness, cradling and crushing me gently in arms of sorrow and misery so tightly I couldn't breathe, nor did I want to. The centre of my universe was gone.

And I went insane.

I know, I know: I was already insane. I've always been insane. But it was different. I can't really describe the difference. Maybe it was more…complete? I had no touch whatsoever with our shared reality for several months, while before, I shared what everyone else around me was seeing and hearing; I just saw and heard them differently. Not anymore. Everything made sense, finally. There were no questions. I knew the truth. I was a walking curse, damning those I loved because I'd no business loving when I didn't deserve to be loved.

By loving, I was demanding love in return, and that wasn't allowed. I killed my wife by loving her. I'd made a horrible mistake, and Dixie paid the price. I had, of course, always known I had no value, but I could fight that thought with my service to others. This proved it irrefutably, in all its stark truth. I was unlovable and undeserving of love and unwanted and worthless and valueless. I had now found my rightful place in the world: utterly alone.

Something like that, I think. It's hard to remember it now with any detail. Before, I wore several masks to put the image people expected to see in front of them. Everyone in Edmonton would be shocked to know they never saw the real me. Everyone in

Calgary would be shocked to hear the people in Edmonton describe me.

Now I didn't need a mask. People wanted nothing to do with me, and that was as it should be. I welcomed that separation, for the universe was even more dangerous than before. The world was tied together by her unbearable absence from everywhere. She wasn't just missing from my house. She'd been everywhere with me for twenty years. Always present in my mind and in my heart, and now she was nowhere. So I didn't need my mind or my heart anymore. If she was nowhere, when she used to be everywhere, what use had I for the things I used to hold her in?

She'd been my everything, and now, with her gone, all that was left was Nothing. The Nothing. How was I to deal with the worst pain of my life when the only person I had to speak with about these things was gone? How could I cope with her loss when I always had her to hold me together? What was I to do with that? The only person who could have helped me deal with her death was her, and she was gone. Forever. From everywhere. I had an injury that somehow took away its own cure.

Then, because I fell in love with Dennette less than a year after, some people judged me, decided I didn't love Dixie, decided I wasn't grieving properly. Which made me worse, as I, too, thought I was a piece of shit. Some people thought because I fell in love, I was all better. Cured from grief.

They were wrong. Turns out, you can be in love and in pain at the same time. I was multi-tasking. Poorly.

And I spent the next five years hiding my grief from Dennette because I didn't want to hurt her, except that's not quite true. I tried to hide my grief from myself. That's as much as I can do right now.

41

TO MY SONS #12

In which our hero provides advice intent on guiding us toward mental well-being.

My sons, don't do things you hate. If possible, find a way to make a living doing what you love to do. But that isn't always possible, so at the very least, just don't waste your time and efforts doing things you honestly despise. It'll only surround your mind with negative thoughts. It took me years to find the courage to do the thing I loved, and in those years, I did many things I hated doing. Not one was worth an ounce of labour or a moment of thought. My insecurities kept me from enlisting until I was an old man of twenty-four, when my only dream from the age of four was to be a commando. My years as a paratrooper were everything I hoped they'd be.

After my medical discharge, I became a corrections officer, and I hated almost every second of it, but I was so lost in trauma and fear, I stayed in the most poisonous environment I've ever encountered—a decade of misery but too scared to accept a new challenge. Learn from my cowardice, and learn from my success. Do what you love, and if you can get paid to do it, even better. Just don't settle and get yourself trapped in a job you hate.

Any task, if you look at it from an overall perspective, can seem too big to accomplish, so just watch the foot in front of you. You can't climb a mountain in one shot; you have to break it into steps. Mission plans are broken down into phases. No matter what the job, if you break it down into manageable chunks, it becomes easier to visualize accomplishing and therefore becomes easier to accomplish.

That's how to beat life's challenges: never quitting, always trying, and winning small battles every day. You're going to fall, often, but you've got to stand back up every time. Progress doesn't have to be giant leaps. Small steps are still forward movement. When teaching you to ride your bike, your mom and I told you to look where you want to go. It's the same with all things in life: look forward. Don't spend too much time looking back; you're not going that way.

Your mother and I have tried to teach you to be self-reliant and courageous. We've tried to equip you with the confidence and courage to tackle any challenge, while giving you the tools to deal with adversity and defeat. The best gift I can give you is the power of trying. I can shelter and protect you for as long as I live, but what happens after my death? It's far better for you that I try to make you as capable and confident as I can.

Say and do only those things you can look back upon with pride and others will look upon with respect. That way lies honour. Looking back upon acts you regret causes guilt and shame. That way lies insanity.

You are the people you associate with. If you hang around with people who lack honour, it's because you've chosen to throw away yours. If you associate with people who have no character, it's because you have none. Choose to surround yourself only with people who demand your best and enhance your life. Associate only with people who challenge themselves and comport themselves with honour.

Just as you must first be afraid to be courageous, so must you admit ignorance to gain knowledge and be foolish to gain wisdom. The fool never learns because he's too afraid to appear foolish and so never admits he doesn't know. That fear prevents him from asking those who know; thus, he never knows.

Wisdom comes from mistakes, and mistakes come from doing foolish things. I dunno how wise I may be, but I've made many mistakes because I've been a fool, and I've spent much time gathering knowledge. I love you.

42

GRIEF #2

In which our hero explains the process of grief and advice on helping the bereaved.

I tried to tell myself, "This is your new normal; get used to it." But I didn't. Instead, I did what I'd always done. I pushed the feeling down, just as I had with every other emotion I didn't know how to process.

Some bereaved go through a denial phase where they expect to see the deceased again. Not me. I didn't deny her death. I tried to deny what her loss did to me. I pushed the knowledge I was completely insane away. I kept trying to be the man I thought everyone wanted me to be, but I never was that man, and it got harder and harder.

My insanity wouldn't allow me to just ask for help. I don't need any fucking help. I'm hard. I'm strong. I'm not weak. And the nightmare continued, with my needs demanding two opposing things at the same time.

Grief makes you feel totally powerless. Or maybe it just points it out, really. Because we're all going to die. We're all dying this very second. We all began to die the instant we were conceived. And we spend all our efforts in denying that. We hide our elderly away in comfortable prisons so we never have to be reminded we, too, will get old.

Some bereaved feel powerless because the person they loved was taken away. I felt powerless because I was experiencing emotions I didn't want: sorrow, grief, pain, sadness, loneliness. I felt powerless because I felt. I'd devoted years to not feeling.

So, since I didn't want to feel pain, because that's weakness, I got angry and did shit. Rage is my default setting for any situation. Rage makes you strong. (That's a lie, by the way. Anger is almost never a primary emotion. It's almost always a secondary emotion that masks the primary. The primary is usually fear, either physical or psychological.)

So I got busy, giving everything away so I wouldn't burden anyone with my possessions when I killed myself, cracking jokes that were actually screams for help nobody could hear. I don't even remember everything I was doing, to be honest. I don't remember much of the first six months at all. But action, movement, was my solution.

Except it wasn't. Not at all. No matter how busy I got, I was still there, and so was the shit I didn't want to think about. Nothing I did made the pain go away. Because I never did the one thing I needed to do: sit in the feeling, let it run its course, and then let it go. Y'know, feel emotions. I didn't allow that. Hadn't for years. Maybe ever, I don't know.

I'd lost my only emotional outlet. I knew I shouldn't love her, or accept her love, because I was a worthless creature, undeserving of love. I cherished her love, gloried in it, bathed in it, but knew it had to end because I didn't deserve it. Anyway, it was gone, and I was truly where I belonged: alone.

I was already crazy with sadness and loneliness and self-loathing. Now it'd come to its proper fruition. I deserved it. I deserved the pain to make up for...well, for existing. Her slow, painful death, lost in her pain and loneliness was the punishment I deserved for daring to believe I could have happiness. I killed her. It was my fault she was dead, and I needed to follow her.

And almost nobody knew what I needed or how to give it to me.

Here's some shit you need to know so you can help the ones you care about when they grieve. Mourners are as lost to the world as the dead themselves. We're dead inside, but it's temporary. How temporary depends on many factors, but your behaviour and attitude toward us will influence that timeframe.

Don't pressure the bereaved to carry on as they were before. "Before" is gone for them. Just be there for them. It's the same as with addiction, depression, anxiety, or PTSD. The cure is connection. Even when you don't know what to say, you don't have to say anything. We probably don't want to, or can't, hear the words anyway. We almost certainly won't remember them later.

Just sit with them. In silence. It may be uncomfortable silence for you, but it's a way to connect to them. They need it. You can do it. Let's leave it there for now. That's a hopeful note to end on.

43

TO MY SONS #13

In which our hero gives us lessons on the importance of self-esteem and self-care.

My sons, my job isn't to tell you to do things but to tell you how to do things. My role is to tell you how to do things that will enhance your life and in such a way that the doing of them further enhances your life. Hopefully I've done so in such a way you happily choose to include me in your life, because the both of you enhance mine immeasurably.

If you don't know that fire exists, you'll eat raw food and freeze your entire life. First, I have to show you fire exists. Second, I have to show you fire can burn you. I can tell you until I'm blue in the face that fire will burn you, but until you feel heat and burn yourself a little bit, you don't know what "hot" and "burn" mean. I can show you burnt things and explain what fire did, but you may not be able to grasp the reality of fire's dangers from concepts and ideas.

I have to let you feel heat and maybe even burn yourself a

little, standing by with cold water and clean dressings, just in case. Then I have to teach you how to use fire safely. Once you understand what fire is and how to utilize it safely, you'll never freeze or eat uncooked food. Life is fire. I hope I'm showing you how to use it well.

Self-care is important. I've exercised strenuously for many years and eaten fairly cleanly. None of this was in the interest of self-care. I didn't care about me, so I had no interest in self-care. I trained my body and ate healthy to be dangerous. To be able to harm others more efficiently and to be as imposing as possible, in hopes of frightening potential foes. Fitness was another avenue my mental illness strolled down to keep control of me. That has changed, thanks to therapy, thanks to you.

I've always been able to be kind to everyone but me. That has changed in recent months, with my leaving the jail and allowing my brain to heal. I've spent these months breathing, and I've finally allowed a valuable lesson to take root that my therapist has tried to teach me: treat yourself with the same care you'd give someone in your care. My boys, you're as responsible for taking care of yourselves as you will be of your own children in time.

It took my having children to learn this. Thank you. I love you.

44

GRIEF #3

In which our hero explains how grief is another form of mental illness.

So…yeah, grief is unique to every individual because every individual has unique experiences. Same with any form of trauma. That's why when an awful thing happens to two people, one's fine, the other's fucked. Same with grief.

Grief's universal. Everybody's going to go through it. Everybody's going to survive someone they love. You're all going to grieve, so pay fucking attention and maybe you won't go through what I did.

When I was lost, not just in grief, but in trauma and everything else, I knew it was permanent. It was forever. There was no way out (well, there was one way out, but we've covered suicide elsewhere, I think). So, yeah, grief, pain, was unbearable, so I didn't bear it. I ran.

I fled into crazy and pulled the tunnel in behind me. Life was nearly unbearable when I had her to help me. I couldn't see then, yeah, life was never going to be the same, but it could be good. Y'see, by that time, I couldn't recall a time when life was ever good. I couldn't remember ever being happy, with the shit I'd done to myself and had done to me, not least of which was watching her die day by day.

For years, we could carry the other's baggage, but I went through one thing too many, or maybe she did, or maybe it was both of us at the same time...I don't know for sure. But we were both lost in our own pain, and the dynamic shifted, and we couldn't help the other, so we were both totally alone. So she retreated into her pain as I did the same.

And she died. Took her two years, but it happened. Every day, as I left the house, I'd wonder, "Will I come home to her or to her corpse?" Every night, "Will I wake up beside her or her corpse?" You think you'll be ready. You aren't. Trust me.

Anyway, grief, like any other mental illness or trauma, makes you do and say really stupid shit. Because you're bananas. Your brain's in shock. It tries to deal with the current situation by drawing on past experiences. Well, I had nothing like this in my past because I didn't love anybody else like that, never mind have them leave me forever. So I did and said things that made no sense. (Fun tip: if someone you love is doing and saying things that make no sense, help them; don't judge them. Jus' sayin'.)

I tried to go on the same as I was before, to be strong for everyone else (and make sure they all stayed away) so they wouldn't know I was totally lost and helpless. And people didn't know what to make of it, so they accused me of not grieving properly, or not loving her, or being glad she was dead so I could have affairs, or whatever. I was screaming for help, but in a way nobody could hear.

Anyway, I learned the hard way I could do two things at once. I could be totally lost in pain and misery and depression and madness, and still laugh. And I could love again.

And that was a bitch to try and accept. I was ashamed of myself for loving someone new, no matter how amazing that person was. I shouldn't be able to feel this again, especially now. I'm a piece of shit. Proof I'm a worthless creature, right there. Underserving of both Dixie's and Dennette's love.

How can I feel any joy in life when everything that mattered is gone? What kind of piece of shit am I, exactly? To love someone and feel like I'm cheating on both of them. To feel love when I shouldn't be able to. And then, to have a child...total grief and total love...I couldn't reconcile these two polar opposites. I couldn't cope. So I didn't. I fled into insanity. Took years to get through all this shit. PTSD, depression, anxiety, new trauma piled onto old trauma, and grief...there's actually more, but that's all we'll discuss for now.

I think it's enough; don't you?

45

THE BEREAVED #1

In which our hero advises us what happens when we grieve.

How do you help the bereaved? Especially the ones who "aren't" mourning? (They are, you know.) But we have to "keep a stiff upper lip" and "be strong" and all that bullshit that leads us all to mental illness by denying our emotions, which means we're denying our humanity, which is fucking crazy. So, how do you help the bereaved, especially if it's a man, most especially if it's a tough-guy, uber-macho, paratrooper-cowboy-biker, overcompensating-for-deep-seated-insecurities-hiding-his-grief-and-pain-because-that's-weakness-and-I'm-not-fucking-weak man, like me?

Show up. That's how. Just show up, man. Don't judge if you think they're doing or saying things that don't match your idea of grieving. Be empathetic. Keep showing up, especially when they try to push you away by saying stupid shit like "I'm okay." No matter how well they camouflage their grief and look like they got their shit wired tight, it's a mask.

I couldn't let anybody know how weak I felt. If I did, if I let them see how much pain I was in and how much I desperately needed somebody, they'd know I was weak. And if they knew, then I'd have to face it myself because I couldn't deny it. I couldn't deny I was a human being with human emotions and had been damaged and needed to do work to fix my shit because that's weak. (Wow, what a culture we've created, huh? Being human is weakness.) And if I faced my "weakness," I had to face my pain and deal with it, and no way was I going to face my pain. I'd spent years not facing my demons; no way was I going to face this one!

So, in the midst of all that, I knew what people wanted from me. They wanted to see me "being strong" and "pushing through" and "moving on" and "getting over it," and fuck that. I wasn't "being strong"; I was hiding my grief. I "pushed" alright, pushed everyone away. I haven't "moved on." That means I left something behind, and I don't want to leave her behind. So I moved forward. Brought her with me, though. And you don't "get over" the death of the person you love; you get through it. But I knew everyone wanted to see that, and if they did, they'd leave me alone, and if they left me alone, they couldn't see my weakness.

So I put on my tough-guy mask and faked it. No way was I going to be vulnerable. That takes too much real courage and true strength.

I lied. With my everything. Because I was scared. Scared to be human. Scared of judgment (boy did that backfire, huh?). Anyway, whatever, we've covered that ground.

Yeah, when you grieve, you'll learn you will also feel happiness,

and love, and other gross, gooey emotions along with the awfulness you expect or even believe you should. It's okay. It's okay.
Whatever your brain does when you mourn is just like whatever
it does when you're exposed to traumatic events, whatever it
has to. It's okay. Let it do what it must in order to process the
pain and recover. The more you fight it, the worse it gets. Ask
me how I know.

Grief is insanity. At least it was for me. But then, I was already
insane, so this was just the very last straw.

Okay, so when it happens to you, here's some shit to know. You
can and will feel positive emotions along with all the negative
ones, and that's okay. You will do and say some weird shit, and
that's okay. Grief will come in waves whenever it wants, stay
for as long as it wants, and want to leave; let it. Let it go; it'll
come back. Don't worry. Letting go of the pain isn't letting go
of the person. Letting go of the pain isn't forgetting them. It's
just letting go of the pain. It never really gets easy, but it does
get easier. Don't be ashamed of your tears. Tears just mean you
loved someone, and there's no shame in love.

Love hard. Love as hard as you can, because one day it's gone.

46

TO MY SONS #14

In which our hero lays out reading material that will guide the mind toward mental health.

My sons, I hope I've sent you to good schools and you've learned your lessons well, but these institutions don't teach you all there is and quite often tell you lies in the name of ideology. Educate yourselves. Don't let school get in the way of your education.

I cannot recommend enough you read Theodore Roosevelt's "Citizenship in a Republic" speech. I can say it no better than he did.

Read William Ernest Henley's poem "Invictus"; read "Ithaka," by C. P. Cavafy and Marcus Aurelius's *Meditations*.

Read *Animal Farm* and *1984*, by George Orwell, and *Lord of the Flies*, by William Golding, to see how power corrupts.

Read *Starship Troopers*, by Robert A. Heinlein, to understand how democracy can stand in the face of corruption.

Dylan Thomas said it for me in his poem "Do Not Go Gentle into That Good Night," as did Rudyard Kipling in "If," and Max Ehrmann in "Desiderata."

Read the works of John Stuart Mill, John Adams, and Jeremy Bentham to understand the value and fragility of liberty.

Read Homer's *Iliad* to learn of the horror and futility of war, and the glory and joy of individual combat: the curse of my kind.

Go to the bookshelf in the den; read both collections of Thomas Bulfinch, one on mythology and the other on chivalry. These books will sweep you away in adventure, and I encourage it, my boys.

Beside them, you'll find autobiographies of Chuck Norris and Georges St-Pierre.

Read *The Three Musketeers*, by Alexandre Dumas, to learn the importance of loyalty and to just have some serious fun.

Read *The Adventures of Tom Sawyer*, by Mark Twain (then find everything he's ever written and enjoy his wisdom and his wit), to realize how our society lies to itself about how children's lives are innocent and idyllic. I hope I've made yours as much so as possible.

Mary Shelley's *Frankenstein* will demonstrate how humanity constantly seeks technological advancement yet fears the changes it inevitably brings.

Ray Bradbury's *Fahrenheit 451* predicted how mass media would be the bane of humanity. He couldn't even begin to imagine the horrors of social media.

Jack London's *The Call of the Wild* and *White Fang* are great stories about toughness and courage and how dogs are just better people than humans.

Heart of Darkness, by Joseph Conrad, gives a different perspective on colonialism and therefore a lesson in seeing the world through different lenses.

To understand why half of your family is the way it is, read *Seven Fallen Feathers*, by Tanya Talaga, *Clearing the Plains*, by James Daschuk, *The Inconvenient Indian*, by Thomas King, and *21 Things You May Not Know about the Indian Act*, by Bob Joseph.

Heed the wisdom in the "Hávamál," Bruce Lee's *Tao of Jeet Kune Do*, Sun Tzu's *The Art of War*, Miyamoto Musashi's *The Book of Five Rings*, and *Hagakure*, by Yamamoto Tsunetomo.

I speak to you often of persistence and resiliency. These ideals cannot be exemplified better than in Homer's *Odyssey*, J.R.R. Tolkien's *Lord of the Rings* trilogy, and Louis L'Amour's Sackett novels.

William Shakespeare was a brilliant psychologist, and he'll teach you humanity's foibles and foolishness.

Edgar Rice Burroughs's *Barsoom* series taught me much of the power of dreams and honour.

Read everything by Gabor Maté and Brené Brown on the

bookshelf. Read *The Body Keeps the Score*, by Bessel van der Kolk; *The Power of Attachment*, by Diane Heller; LCol David Grossman's books *On Killing* and *On Combat*; and *The Grief Recovery Handbook*, by John James and Russell Friedman, so you can understand why your brain does the shit it does.

Sir Arthur Conan Doyle led me to understand the importance of using your head for more than an oddly shaped hat rack; read his Sherlock Holmes collection.

You'll find it beside Robert E. Howard's collection of Conan stories on the bookshelf near the headboard of our bed. Conan, too, will teach you the importance of using your mind as well as the strength of your limbs. For that matter, Sherlock Holmes teaches you the same.

Read the New Testament and the Pāli Nikāyas to hear the wisdom of Jesus of Nazareth and the Gautama Buddha. Perhaps they were divine, perhaps not, but they had some very good ideas, and they both said the same thing: treat everyone as you'd want to be treated in turn.

Read Confucius's *Analects* and compare it to Plato's *Republic*, then contrast both with *Black Elk Speaks*, by John G. Neihardt.

School will try to tell you what to think. Read things that will teach you how to think and inspire you to think. I love you.

47

MIRRORS AND WINDOWS

In which our hero allegorically describes the poor self-image of those with mental illness.

I get shit mixed up sometimes, hell, all the time.

People I try to help do the same, and the things they say about themselves is...well, it's total bullshit, to be honest.

I think I figured out why.

When I look at my shit, I'm looking in a mirror.

In a mirror, everything's backwards, and you can't see much, depending on the size of the mirror.

When I look at you, I'm looking through a window.

I see everything right way 'round, and I see way more than you can in your mirror.

I don't see everything, of course.

I can't see into the corners where the angle's wrong and it's all dark, but I see more than you do, and I see it right way 'round.

So trust me when I say you're worth a damn and deserve to allow yourself to be loved.

I see it clearer than you do.

48

MOLON LABE

In which our hero describes his inner battle with suicidal thoughts.

I am at war.

My enemy is relentless.

Merciless.

And he hates me.

I don't know why he hates me so very much.

But he does.

There will never be peace.

He won't allow a truce.

He doesn't rest.

He never gets tired.

The more exhausted I get, the stronger he becomes and the fiercer he attacks.

He will never stop until he kills me.

No matter what I do, I cannot seem to kill him.

He's cunning and knows all my weaknesses.

Where to strike.

When I am at my weakest.

What weapon will cause the most pain.

He comes for me in the night.

He attacks when I sleep.

His attacks are just as savage when I am awake and think I am prepared for him.

It's exhausting to face that kind of hatred, day in and day out.

To be under siege all day.

Every day.

All night.

Every night.

There are times when all I can do is bring in the sentries, hole up, and try to wait out the storm of hate that comes at me.

Times when I realize I've been flanked again, he's achieved defilade and has me in enfilade again.

There are times when I'm so tired of the fight, I want nothing more than to surrender, just to make it stop.

Because if I win, it's never for good.

He doesn't quit.

He will never stop.

Every time I win a battle, it's just so I can fight again tomorrow.

But I can't quit.

If he wins, my family loses.

So I fight.

And will again tomorrow.

And every tomorrow after that.

He fights because he hates.

I fight because I love.

I have to believe that means I will win.

Molon labe, motherfucker.

Come get some.

49

THE BEREAVED #2

In which our hero explains how to help those in mourning.

News flash: you can't take away a mourner's pain. You can't fix grief unless you can bring the dead back. You can, however, show up and do work. With that, here's some shit not to say:

"At least they aren't in pain any longer..." True. But I am, asshole! All "at least" did was demean my pain and belittle my loss. Don't say this, okay? Let the mourner have the dignity of their grief and loss. It's not about the deceased; it's about the mourner. Focus.

"Everything happens for a reason." Oh really? What possible reason is there for me to be in this much pain, you fucking asshole? Everything doesn't happen for a reason. Shitty things happen, and everybody dies, and that's life, so don't spew this drivel to somebody in mourning, okay? This crap just invalidated my emotions, and I was struggling enough with them on my own.

"They wouldn't want you to…" Stop. Shut your hole right now. You don't know what they'd want; you don't know my relationship; you don't know shit. Shut up. You don't get to tell me how to grieve or what to feel. Telling me Dixie wouldn't want me to mourn forever was a fucking insult. As a matter of fact, she would want me to mourn forever because she wanted me to love her forever. Grief and love are the same thing. You don't grieve the absence of something you didn't love.

"I know how you feel." Oh really? Way to make it all about you, asshole. How about shut your cakehole, get over yourself for a minute, and focus on helping me through my pain? Maybe you've experienced grief, but you aren't experiencing my grief. If you want to empathize, that's great, but you don't know how I feel. You know how you felt. Stick to that wording, okay?

"It's God's plan." Oh boy. I'm glad your faith gives you comfort. Trust me on this: doesn't matter what your religion is, unless you know it's also the mourner's, keep your trap shut. I'm not a Christian, and Dixie was an avowed atheist. Saying it's "God's plan" to another Christian is a great way to say "God" hates them; he's hurting them so badly, it must be punishment. Good job, buds. Kick 'em in the crotch while you're at it. Poke 'em in the eye.

Saying nothing = unhelpful. I get it. You don't wanna say the wrong thing, so you don't say anything. That felt like you didn't give a shit. Y'know what I wanted to hear? "She'll be missed." I wanted to know the entire world was sharing my pain and everyone knew the world was dark and lonely without her. "I remember when…" I wanted to know her memory was going to live on with everyone. Try those sorts of things when it's your turn to help a mourner, okay?

To those who judged me: I forgive you. I didn't know what I didn't know either. We're all learning together.

50

YOU ARE LOVED

In which our hero addresses seasonal depression added to the pandemic of 2020.

Yule is upon us. And the world's a giant too-full box of kitty litter.

It's easy to slip away in times like this.

Go back to the darkness, where we can suffer in the comfort of familiarity.

We can numb out. Go blank. Not feel.

Doesn't matter how horrible the darkness is or how much our demons torment us there.

We know it. It's comfortable. In a sick, demented way, it's safe, even.

We can have that drink or use our chemical of choice to hide from that shit. Right?

No. No, it's incorrect.

It isn't factual, and we all know it.

I get it. I'm feeling it. I'm right there too.

But it's not true. It just isn't, and you know I'm right.

Hell, even I know I'm right, and I never believe my own bullshit.

Our demons are scary and fierce and relentless.

But they can't defeat us, you know. They can't. They can only win if we surrender.

As long as you're still fighting, they're losing and you're winning.

So don't quit on me. I need you around to hate next year with me too.

The world's scary as fuck right now, with the shitty media and the shittier politicians competing to see who can scare us more with lies and half-truths.

It's okay to be confused, and confusion breeds fear.

It's okay to be scared. You can't be brave until you've been afraid.

Courage is being scared and doing what needs doing anyway. Ya gotta be scared to be brave.

But you're not alone. We're all taking a bite out of the same shit sandwich.

You're loved. I know this to be true because I know there are people you love so much, you'd die for them. That tells me there are people who feel the same fucking way about you.

You're not alone. You're loved. You have value.

When the demons come, there are people who'll fight them with you.

I know a guy. Reach out. I've no fear of your demons.

I'm far too busy being terrified of mine.

The world's a better place with you in it. Stay on this side of the snow.

Be kind.

Kindness creates strength and courage, and it's contagious.

51

TO MY SONS #15

In which our hero reiterates previous lessons about preventing or fighting mental illness.

My sons, when I couldn't see success in our future, I was reminded to look at the successes of my past. Then I started to do work. Do the same. In times of trial, try. It's okay not to excel at everything you do. You'll almost never excel at something you've never done before. You'll sometimes do some things badly for your entire life. (Ask your mom about my dancing.) Do them anyway. It's better to do something badly than to not do it because of fear. Life rewards planned risk, effort, and enthusiasm.

Be true to your values. Remain humble. No matter how high in life you may rise, treat everyone the same, and be who you are. An honest man doing honest work deserves more respect than a wealthy dirtbag. Be as polite to your server or the cashier or the janitor as you'd want to be treated. Character's revealed in how you treat others, especially those you could get away with being an asshole to. Give respect first and you'll get respect in return. Demand respect and you'll never get it, because you don't deserve it.

One of the most important lessons about life I've learned is struggle is good. If you don't struggle from time to time, you're either coasting or settling. Nobody brags about the easy things they've done. Those fools that do get ignored or mocked. You boast of the difficult things you've accomplished. Struggle is good. My struggles have brought me to a place where I can use the lessons I've learned about mental illness and grief and addiction to help others stuck back where I was. Struggle is growth. Life is struggle. A life without struggle is stagnation. Stagnation is rot. A living death. Learning is struggle. Enjoy it. Be grateful for it. Be inspired by it.

Choose to be positive. Choose to give out positive energy. Look back with an eye for the positive. I used to define myself by my failures. Don't do that. It's stupid. That person isn't you anymore. That's yesterday you. You're today you, this person right here and right now. You can choose to learn from your mistakes. Reassess, reload, reorg, re-cock, and re-attack. Create positive energy by using the inspiration and gratitude you have for the good results from the choices you've made. Use every positive result from every good decision you make to build your confidence. Positive energy creates positive results.

Don't waste energy on negativity. Don't dwell on your mistakes; just learn from them, and move on. Don't let another's success make you bitter or envious. These are petty emotions that sap your energy and cause you to waste your time thinking about someone else. Poor losers are losers because they choose to be poor about it. Anyone who wastes their time hating on another because that other is successful is a failure. They'll always be a failure because their energy is diluted and they can't focus. Haters are losers. They hate because they lose, and they lose because they waste their energy hating. Don't waste energy on envy; choose instead to be inspired by another's success.

I've been mediocre in my life. I know well that feeling of shame for lack of effort. That feeling of shame for laziness, for not trying out of insecurity. Don't do that. Ask yourself, "What would a person I admire do? What would a person I respect do? What would the person I want to be do right now?" Then do that. You can do it. I know this. I love you.

52

RANDOM ADVICE #2

In which our hero cautions us to avoid the common pitfall of trying to help others too soon.

I got some advice: if you're broken, you ain't fixin' nobody.

If you're drowning, you can't throw nobody a lifeline.

Why're you picking up the trash in somebody else's yard when yours is a dumpster fire?

There's a reason the stewardess says put the oxygen mask on yourself first.

Learned that shit the hard way, so I know it's true.

Spent years trying to straighten out other people when I was all kinds of broken.

Loyalty's great. I'm loyal as a dog. Everybody knows that.

And dogs are awesome. Everybody knows that. But they ain't ever fixed nobody.

If everybody in your family's a psychological train wreck, you think you got out unscathed?

If everybody you know is nuts, there's a common denominator.

Check yourself. Jus' sayin'.

53

DEAR SHERIDAN #1

In which our hero encourages himself after yet another setback on his journey to mental health.

Dear Sheridan,

It's okay not to be okay.

Normal is a setting on your washing machine. It doesn't apply to people. It doesn't apply to you.

Your life doesn't come with conditions. Your worth is intrinsic; it doesn't depend on others.

You deserve it. To be content. To feel calm. To be at peace. To feel joy. To be happy.

Fate will often save a man, when his courage holds.

If you want to get ahead, you'd better get started.

You can't be defeated if you never quit.

Failing is as necessary for success as fear is for courage.

Learn from yesterday; don't try to live there. Use yesterday's lessons today to make tomorrow less hellish.

Love hard.

Decide today's going to be a good day, and it probably will be.

It's hard to be depressed and grateful at the same time.

They're all wrong; the glass is neither half full nor half empty. It's fucking refillable.

Good things don't come to those who wait. Those who wait get what's left. Are you an eagle or a vulture?

Hard times can make you harder or break you. Decide.

Genghis Khan, da Vinci, Edison, Rockefeller all had twenty-four hours in a day, just like you. Don't whine about "enough time."

Be kind. Even to you.

Fall down seven times; stand up eight. Champions are contenders who didn't quit.

How much longer are you gonna criticize yourself? It's been five decades, and you still don't like you yet.

Who do you want to be? Pretend to be him until you are.

Love, Sheridan

54

CURSES AND BLESSINGS

In which our hero speaks on reversing negative thought patterns.

We're given two things in this life: curses and blessings.

We're gifted with curses to learn from, to become wiser and stronger. If we don't heed the lessons in the curses, we break.

Alcohol was a curse. I learned.

Depression was a curse. I learned.

PTSD was a curse. I learned.

Anxiety was a curse. I learned.

Grief was a curse. I learned.

We're given blessings that we may share them. If we don't share the blessings we're gifted with, they become curses we never heal from.

We break.

Here's a secret I've learned: your curse might just be your blessing.

Learn from it. Become wiser.

Then share the lesson. Make your curse your blessing.

55

DEAR SHERIDAN #2

In which our hero encourages himself after yet another setback on his journey to mental health.

More isn't better. Better is better. Endless consumption doesn't equal one act of creation. Stop buying shit you don't need. Go plant a tree.

Stop being weak. Go do something difficult for no reason. Achieve.

Make yourself be comfortable with discomfort. Comfort is stagnation.

Civil disobedience in the face of tyranny is patriotism. Disobey unjust laws.

Spirituality is vital; religion's bullshit. Talk to the Divine Power today and give it your own name. You might as well; it wears your face.

Speak the truth. First to yourself, then to others. You'll feel better, and it's easier than remembering lies.

Keep your word. Say what you mean; mean what you say. People will respect you. You will too.

Helping others enriches their life, your life, and the world.

Be kind. To everyone, you included.

When you allow another to provoke you to anger, you give them power over your mind.

Have a plan and backup plan to deal with life's fuckery because the plan never survives first contact with the enemy.

Mental illness isn't a character defect. You're not weak, immoral, flawed, or worthless because you're struggling. And you're not alone.

Seeking to understand before you seek to be understood prevents miscommunication and misunderstanding.

Smile, for fuck's sake. You'll feel better, and it's contagious.

You got this.

Love, Sheridan

56

FEAR, LIES, AND STATISTICS

In which our hero shows how the fear struggle in society and our minds is the same, and they both need addressing.

The media and government tell you licensed gun owners are responsible for all firearm crime. That's a blatant lie. Licensed firearms owners commit the least crime. Right now, liars are telling you we need more and stricter firearm laws, and if you believe it, you don't understand the already strict laws we comply with.

Here's the thing: if I removed all guns from Earth, would people rob and kill? Well, if I left the guns and took away the people, would people rob and kill? Guns ain't the problem. Despite the media, gun crime is nowhere near the leading cause of death in Canada. The media ignore hundreds of thousands of deaths from cancer, heart disease, stroke, respiratory disease, accidents, diabetes, influenza, and pneumonia. The top causes of death in Canada.

The media focus on the tool of violence instead of the cause of violence. They don't care about victims. If they did, they'd focus on the cause of crime. Take away the cause of crime and the tool doesn't matter. Money wasted chasing duck hunters could be spent housing the homeless and treating addicts. Let's stop punishing innocent people and try to help victims. Jus' sayin'.

Gun crime is already illegal. That's why we call it "crime." Not sure you realize this, but all forms of armed violence are currently, right now, illegal. Doesn't stop criminals from committing crime. They don't obey the law. That's why we call them criminals. There are no laws that prevent crazy people from committing violence. They don't comply with the law because they're not in the same reality we are. That's why we call them crazy.

"Why do you need a gun?" Why do I have to explain why I want to own anything, as long as I harm nobody? Why do you need a car? Automobiles are far and away more dangerous to the public than firearms. Check how many Canadians die from automobiles in a year, and compare it to how many die from firearms. G'head. I'll wait.

Licensed firearms owners have already exemplified they're law-abiding citizens by following the law, hence the phrase "licensed firearms owners." Regulations for licensed firearms owners to remain law-abiding citizens are pretty damn complicated to obey. The fact that licensed firearms owners do follow them all proves they're law-abiding.

Licensed firearms owners hafta go through an eight-hour course on how to handle, store, transport, and use firearms.

It's a sixteen-hour course if they want restricted firearms. Then they can apply for a licence, which is actually a five-year pardon. You see, firearm ownership in Canada is a federal offence. The Possession and Acquisition Licence is a five-year pardon that can be revoked at any time for no reason. Once they apply for the PAL, they get background-checked. If they pass that, they might receive a licence. They're then subject to continuous eligibility checks every day to see if they're a possible threat. You read that correctly: Canadian gun owners are background-checked every single day.

Restricted firearms are registered to the owner. Assault rifles aren't available in Canada, contrary to what you're being told. Assault rifles go brrrpp brrrpp. They're fully automatic. That's part of the definition of "assault rifle." An assault "weapon" is anything you use to commit an assault on someone, be it a firearm or a golf club. Magazine capacity is maxed to five rounds in rifles, ten in handguns. No million-round magazines to go brrrpp brrrpp with.

No loaded guns in the house. Stored firearms must be locked up, and the ammunition has to be stored separately. When transporting restricted firearms, you hafta get an Authorization to Transport, a pain-in-the-ass phone call to an overworked, understaffed office worker for a piece of paper to kill trees and allow you to move your restricted firearm to a licensed range or licensed gunsmith. Straight there, straight back, trigger locked in a locked case. Ammunition has to travel separately in a locked case.

Despite how far firearms owners go to obey the laws, they still get lied about by the media. An article on CBC claimed, "according to police, a growing number of guns are bought legally in Canada and resold on the black market or made here illegally." This is a blatant lie, and all evidence proves the opposite. Only 148 of the 1,740 firearms police seized in 2017 were legally purchased. I did the math for you; it's less than 9 percent. People who legally buy guns don't do it to commit crimes. People who commit crimes don't buy guns legally.

When the government declared their $250 million buyback program (How do you buy back something you never owned? I don't get it), there was a big uptick in crime. (Probably something to do with their lessening sentences for belonging to organized crime or terrorist groups.) Speaking of...that $250 million program? Another lie. The list of firearms banned by the government is almost 10,000. That's over 400,000 firearms bought by responsible people who paid money and used their own time to get trained on how to safely use them.

So that makes the cost of this program waaayyy over $1 billion. You know how many kids you could feed with $1 billion? I wonder how far $1 billion would go toward bringing drinkable water to Reserves in Northern Ontario. Y'know, where all those babies are dying every day?

That was pretty long. If you're still with me, you probably know I don't give a shit if you like or hate guns. This wasn't about firearms. It isn't about honesty or integrity, even though your government isn't displaying any. Nor is it about liberty or democracy, even though your government is trying to remove both. (Look into which government first removed firearm ownership from its citizens. I'll give you a hint: it was the Nazis.

Worked out great, huh? When governments take guns away, it's because they're doing shit people would shoot them for.)

No, this was written about fear and control. As I've come out of my mental illness–induced fog of fear and need for control, I've noticed the same pattern everywhere. Our entire culture is based on fear and control. No wonder we're all fucked up, huh? The crazy guy looks around and sees the whole goddamn country is living the way he was.

Your government is scared of you having control. I'm scared of any government that's scared of their populace having control. They maintain control through fear. Don't allow fear to control you. I let that shit happen to me for years. It was the cause of, and resulted from, insanity. I don't believe people should control other people. That nonsense is how we got to this state of division and hatred. Here's a secret: if you don't try to control other people, you can connect with them.

Wouldn't it be cooler if we all stopped being scared of each other and just talked? If we all stopped letting other people control us through fear and lies? You're being lied to. By your government. Ask why. Check for yourself. Think for yourself. They have you believing you need to obey them, when the reality is they work for you.

It's the same thing with your brain and mental illness. It works for you. Don't let it lie to you and control you with fear. My life was a living fucking hell for years because I did.

57

TO MY SONS #16

In which our hero makes a joke, modelling pride in their heritage to his children to prevent self-esteem issues later.

To my sons: in your veins runs the blood of warriors.

Celtic warriors, Viking warriors, Mi'kmaq warriors, Anishinaabe warriors, and Nehiyawak warriors.

We, my sons, are warriors.

We do as we will.

Where we will.

When we will.

How we will.

But first, we ask your mom.

(We're fierce. We're not stupid.)

58

THE CRITIC

In which our hero explains how judgment underlies mental illness.

In my youth I studied Buddhism, but I'm a fucking terrible Buddhist. I don't suffer well. In my middle years, I've done hundreds of hours of therapy. Because I don't suffer well. Both have taught me to try to let go of anger. Buddhism teaches anger is an unhealthy emotion because it can blind us. Therapy taught me anger is a secondary emotion caused by, and concealing, fear. Usually fear of judgment, and judgment is programmed into us.

I was an angry young man, not knowing why I was angry. I was miserable, festering in the rage in my mind. I was angry, judging myself and finding myself wanting. I was frightened others would see how worthless I was. Fear fed rage, and the cycle continued. I lived in a painful state of never being "good enough," of being "less than." At least I could drink myself into oblivion and forget it all for a moment.

But there's a better way, turns out. When I got flooded with anger (actually fear), due most often to an imagined threat identified by my limbic system, pertaining to my self-image (in other words, I felt judged), I'd be so focused on the emotion that I wouldn't see the trigger that caused the flooding. I couldn't see clearly, so I'd do and say stupidly harmful things out of anger (actually fear). If we take a second to pause, we can make ourselves be present in the now instead of being trapped in the past. That's what trauma is, being trapped in a time of our life we find horribly painful. Ideally, of course, we've put in the work to learn to recognize what our triggers are and why so we can pause when we get triggered or, even better, prevent being triggered.

That critic? The voice in your head saying you're not good enough, not smart enough, not attractive enough? The voice saying you can't, so you don't try? That voice that never shuts up and constantly criticizes you, so you either give up and live in misery, or overcompensate and live in misery? Yeah, that voice comes from a place of negativity programmed into us as a survival mechanism. It comes from the limbic system, and that's why it's so insidious. That part of our brain is oriented toward the negative, programmed toward threat and survival. That voice is part of that survival mechanism.

It starts talking to us in infancy and early childhood, when we're totally dependent on the adults around us for survival. We need to win their approval to have the food we need to survive and the love we need to make life worth living. So we learn to fit in, do as we're told, to get food, shelter, and just as importantly, love and affection. The voice started then, telling us to shut certain behaviours off, stop certain reactions, do whatever we must to please our caregivers.

That voice is the internalized voice of our adult caregivers constantly telling us "no!" It is the voice of our caregivers telling us to stop crying (because it bothers them and they don't have the tools to cope), stop being sad or scared or angry (which is impossible, so we learn we're inherently flawed). We have emotions, but our caregivers tell us we aren't allowed certain emotions, except we can't stop having those emotions, so we're bad. That lesson never goes away.

That is the voice of the critic in our head.

That's where the work comes in. The work gives us the tools to see with clarity and awareness. This allows us to take positive action. To control our reactions rather than allow our emotions to hijack our reactions. We learn to create a buffer zone, a small space in time between the trigger, our thoughts, and our reaction. We get to pause and ask ourselves what we want to do rather than allow the voice to tell us what to do. We can't always shut the voice up, but we can decide how much attention we're going to give it. We learn to recognize when the voice is judging us, and we can act instead of react. Acting is a deliberate choice. Reaction is involuntary, and it seldom goes well in ordinary, day-to-day interactions with other humans.

Get the tools you need to allow yourself to act, not react. Get the tools that allow you to buy the time between fear and reaction so you can deliberately act. I dunno if that's gonna be psychotherapy, yoga, medication, tai chi, mindfulness training, or Zen. That's a you thing. But figure it out. It'll make your life better; I promise you.

You got this.

59

STOP HIDING

In which our hero reminds us therapy is difficult but worthwhile.

The shit you most need to find, you're gonna find where you least wanna look. You know why you can't find the shit you need the most? Because it's tucked back in behind all your demons and skeletons. Shoved way back in the dark, cobwebby corner of your mind.

You can't find it because you've spent so much energy hiding from it. You've been avoiding it with everything you have for as long as you could. You've been denying a part of yourself you need desperately, and now you're miserable because you've just realized how badly you need it. And now it's misplaced. You can't find it because you're scared to go crawl into that corner.

I'm telling you, with all the honesty I have, you can't let go of your demons until you face them. Failed coping mechanisms like rage or denial or intoxicants just keep you from looking in that fucking corner where you need to look, because you're scared of finding the shit you most need. It's a vicious circle, and it can only end when you grab a fucking flashlight (or go old-school and grab a torch, I don't give a shit) and go into that corner. Go in there, past the bullshit you think is so scary, grab all the ugly and pull it into the light.

Drag out the things that happened to you when you were a kid, that aren't your fault because you were a kid but you blame yourself for anyway because you were a kid. Drag out the ugly that happened to you and look at it in the sunlight. It's really not as scary as you thought, you know.

Now go back in there and drag out the ugly shit you did to other people because you were hurting and scared and lonely. You gotta own your shit. You did that. That was you, and you did it, so own it. If you keep denying or suppressing or whatever, you ain't gonna be able to do the next step, and it's the most important.

You gotta let that shit go.

That's the really hard part. We get so used to holding on to our pain and chewing it over and over, huddled up in the dark like a dog with an old bone. But it's weighing you down. You don't need it, so you shouldn't carry it. It's getting in the way. It's why you're trapped in the past. It's why you're stuck and can't move past it. Put it down and walk away.

Look back once in a while to keep your bearings, but don't look longingly backwards; you ain't going that way. It all starts with looking where you don't want to look to find what you've been hiding from. Cowboy up. Do work.

It's not the world's fault you're unhappy; it's yours. Move to a new town; you're still there. Get drunk, get high, whatever; when you come down, you're still there. Gamble, change jobs, cheat on your partner...doesn't matter. You're still right fucking there.

If the world you're living in isn't the world you want to be living in, it's time to examine your own-ass self. Look at yourself, at your strengths and weaknesses, honestly. You may need to enlist someone else's help here. We lie to ourselves constantly.

Look at your morals and values. Are you living according to them? Are you sacrificing tomorrow for an easy today? Embrace the suck; do work; sacrifice today to make tomorrow better.

The world can't make you happy. Only you are responsible for your emotions, so only you can decide how you're gonna feel. The world doesn't give a shit about you, y'know. Nobody really does, except for a very few really important people. The world doesn't owe you shit. You want something to be, it's on you to make it happen. Decide who you wanna be. Decide how you're gonna get there. Now grab a shovel and fucking dig.

60

SOME BROKEN HEARTS NEVER MEND

In which our hero reminds us that recovery isn't rebooting.

Some wounds just never heal. It is what it is. Doesn't mean it's always gonna be as bad as it is right now. Doesn't mean it'll ever not hurt. It's okay. I've spine damage and blown-out knees. I'm losing my hearing (but not my hair or teeth, so fuck it). These are always going to be a part of me now. The same is true of my psychological injuries. The same is true of yours. But this is true, too, y'know. They don't have to define you if you don't want them to. Your emotional wounds aren't you; they're just a part of you. You decide if they're going to be a good part or a bad part. Post-traumatic growth is a real thing.

Dixie's death was probably the most painful of every hurt I've ever experienced. It was a fight just to keep moving, a fight I was losing for a while. I saw no point in continuing to breathe, so I wasn't planning on doing it for much longer. Dennette kinda fucked that up. Now I've reached the point where I don't want to share something with Dixie every single day, like I did the first few years, but I wish to hell she could meet my boys.

Alcoholism was a stone-cold ice-queen bitch; I'll tell the world. I don't crave booze every day anymore. Hardly ever, as a matter of fact. Sometimes. Sometimes I can feel the salivation start if I smell whisky or let myself think about it too much. But I know I have to keep an eye on it. It's snuck up on me three times now, and I don't know how many recoveries I got left. I got a million slips and relapses, but recoveries? I'm not gonna risk it.

That damage to my back and knees too. It's something I always have to consider, and when I don't, it bites me in the ass. I had to give up a great job opportunity because the drive was too long. I have to factor it into everything. Can I shovel the drive? Can I work out? Can I afford to skip a workout, since it might seize me up if I do? How badly am I gonna be lamed up if I carry my son down that hill?

Infidelity. Both being the cheater and being cheated on. The former destroys your soul with shame and guilt and remorse. I've hated myself on a special level for many years now, no matter the justification my bullshit tries to offer up. I hurt someone beyond anything I ever thought possible. That ain't going away. I won't let it. Being cheated on destroyed my ability to trust for years. It's a big part of the isolating behaviour. It caused me to doubt myself and my manhood, and I was already an insecure man-boy. It's a part of me, and it makes me a better husband now. I hope so, anyway. If you've been through this shit, remember, something happened to cause that person to act or react the way they did. If it's out of character, try to understand. Try to see it with some curiosity, not just pain and rage. To betray someone, if it's out of character, is a pretty serious cry for help. How lost is that person in loneliness and pain? Try to ask yourself why and how. Try to get past your own pain. Try to use the tools of connection and empathy so you can make a better relationship than you had.

Actually, not just infidelity, but any form of betrayal, really. Betrayal puts our brain into shock. It rocks us to our core. I feel deeply betrayed by this nation on many levels, not least because it continues to demand its political leadership strip us of our every civil liberty. I believed in the ideals of liberty and justice so fundamentally I spent twenty-six years trying to serve those values. I lost large parts of my physical and mental health serving this nation. Only to watch the citizenry demand a tyranny out of social media-driven fear. Canada, you're welcome for my service; you're entirely undeserving of it. Fuck you very much.

The trauma and mental illness. I don't know if they're two different things, the same thing, or what, exactly, but they're not going anywhere any time soon. They're as much a part of me as my tattoos and broken nose. Every morning, I take my meds. All day, I work to stay regulated. Every night, I take my meds. I attend therapy less often, but I still go. I know I could be triggered by something at any given moment, be taken off on a fucking bad trip straight to the deepest pit of hell that overwhelms me and sends my family into their own hell. I live in fear of fear. I know I may get trapped emotionally in some place I never want to revisit, no longer in the same reality as everyone else.

But these things aren't me. They're part of me, yeah. But I don't let them be me anymore. I gotta step carefully sometimes because my knee wants to buckle if I go down that path. I gotta step carefully sometimes because my brain wants to flip out if I go down that path. That's all it is. You can do the same. I know you can. I believe in you, and I'm usually a pretty good judge of character. Now you start believing in you too.

61

TO MY SONS #17

In which our hero encourages us to continue the struggle to mental health.

To my sons: the gods don't reserve their hardest battles for the strongest warriors.

They create the strongest warriors through the hardest battles.

Never quit.

Swear.

Weep.

Rage.

But never quit.

There are no monsters in any realm as fierce as the ones in our heads.

Only we can see them.

Only we can fight them.

They use fear.

They use deception.

Only courage can overcome them.

Only honesty can defeat them.

Only love will give you the power to find that courage and honesty.

Be brave.

Brave enough to be vulnerable.

Be strong.

Strong enough to be honest.

Love hard.

I've loved harder than any man I know.

It has caused pain.

It has caused fear.

It was worth all of it.

I love you.

62

CHILDREN OF MENTALLY ILL PARENTS

In which our hero explains how mental illness passes down generationally.

The children of mentally ill parents grow up in fear. Even parents who try not to let their illness fuck up their children do exactly that. Such is the nature of mental illness. It can't be helped, and mental illness is contagious, so imagine how much worse it is for kids. Our first seven years psychologically program us unless we work to change it. Now imagine how attachment theory affects children of parents struggling with mental illness.

My sons are the children, grandchildren, great-grandchildren, and great-great-grandchildren of Indigenous veterans. That is four generations of PTSD and trauma. My shit had me completely under control for the first three years of my older son's life. My greatest fear is I've scarred him emotionally and caused him to suffer from anxiety. I can't let go of that fear despite being told it isn't true from psychologists and teachers.

The children of ill parents know their parents are different. Maybe it's school, whatever, but they realize their parents are different pretty early, they just can't understand how. Kids can't really grasp mental illness, and they can't separate the parent from the illness. We explain it to the boys as wolves in my brain fighting for control. They seem to grasp the imagery. My son shocked me out of an episode once, asking if the angry wolf was winning. I realized what was happening and dragged my ass into the present. Then I cried for exposing him to that again. Then I dragged my ass out of the shame that created and hugged my kid.

Ill parents ignore their kids' physical and emotional needs because they're trapped in the hell of their own minds. I remember my mother-in-law holding my son, him reaching for a hug. I just stood there, staring at him. Part of my brain was screaming, "Hug my kid!" but my arms wouldn't move. I just drove off, weeping. See the connection with attachment issues? Mental illness gets in the way of being as good a parent as you could.

It's cyclical. I didn't have the relationship with my parents I saw other kids have. I was scared of my parents and their unpredict-ability. Now I dread I've programmed the same damage into my son despite psychologists saying he's fine.

Ill parents don't really talk about the illness with their kids. Always the goddamn stigma, the fear of judgment. The children of ill parents learn from example not to talk about the illness. Some are even explicitly told by a parent, the ill one or the healthier one, not to talk about it, and thus stigma continues. Some children of ill parents are ashamed by their parents' behaviour, so they don't talk about it, even to people who could help, because they've learned to fear judgment. This is no doubt part of why I didn't seek help to deal with Dixie's eating disorder and depression. I'd learned to protect the secret of mental illness, and so my wife died of starvation.

Some children of ill parents worry about their parents' self-neglect and potential or actual self-harm. They become "parentalized" (that's not really a word, but fuck it, it works), leaving them scarred forever. Kids shouldn't be raising their parents or younger siblings.

They might've suffered anger and abuse from their parents, leaving them scarred forever. They might've suffered worse, if their parents self-medicate with intoxicants, leaving them scarred forever. The worst is, as children are all tiny little narcissists, with the universe revolving around them, they blame themselves for their parents' behaviour. Now they've learned to carry more shame because of the fear of stigma and judgment.

The children of ill parents feel isolated from their family, other kids, their total social world. They're ashamed, lonely, and "different" from other kids. Other kids, even mean-spirited adults, will make fun of them and their parents. It's why I scrap as well as I do, I suppose. It's no doubt a big part of why I felt perpetually alone, no matter who was around me. It was habitual, I guess. I'd always been alone, and so was always alone.

We've talked about how mental illness tries to isolate the ill person, to have control of them; well, it does the same thing to their kids. If their kids are locked out, they can't help their parent. Then illness transmits. All the ugly shit we talked about takes over the kid, and bam! It's fucking contagious. I had trust and intimacy issues before I ever had a relationship, and my first relationship choices were unwise. But then, I was alone anyway.

The children of ill parents don't know what a healthy relationship is, so don't know how to create one. They recreate the disastrous relationship of their parents, where trust and intimacy are impossible, thus becoming a self-perpetuating cycle of mistrust and continued mental illness. Remember, the only cure, really, is feeling connected with an emotionally supportive and trustworthy person who validates our emotional needs.

The children of ill parents are terrified of inheriting their parents' mental illness. Many, if not most, have their own struggles with addiction, depression, and anxiety in adolescence and adulthood, if not starting right in early childhood. I don't know how much of it is inherited and how much is taught. I think it's probably a complex interplay of nature and nurture. But it seems to almost inevitably become a self-fulfilling prophecy. "I don't want to be crazy like my parent, so I'll focus all my energy on their crazy, and...wait...why am I crazy?"

63

FAILED COPING MECHANISMS #2

In which our hero revisits mental programming.

Here are more failed coping mechanisms thrust upon me by my crazy.

First and foremost is emotional avoidance, suppression, denial, all that shit. We teach our children they aren't allowed to feel anger, sadness, fear, discouragement, grief, or apprehension, or be in any way unhappy. Which really means we don't know how to cope with their emotions because we were never taught to understand our own, so we get scared and angry. We tell our kids they aren't allowed to feel. Except they're human, so they've no choice but to feel. So they think there's something inherently wrong with them as humans.

I realized this over a span of a couple years. I remember my older son crying, and my anxiety took the wheel. I was in a position where my child needed guidance in handling big emotions and a safe caregiver. And I failed him. My anxiety chose instead to yell at him in my command voice. I still see his beautiful, tiny face overcome with fear. I still feel the shame. And still my anxiety wouldn't let go. It kept me angry, overcompensating for insecurity-driven fear.

Last year, he insulted his mother, and my anxiety took over about halfway through my trying to do the right things. So I did something stupid. I told him to go to his room (because solitary confinement is so effective and healthy). After a couple minutes, I gripped my shit and went up to talk with him. Told him to come out. He said he couldn't; he was still angry.

He didn't make the connection, explicitly laid out for him as it was, that we were angry because he insulted his mother (stupid fucking reason to be angry). He believed he was being punished (fucking stupid thing to do) because he felt anger. He thought Mommy and Daddy were mad at him because he felt an emotion. We've been working on reversing that, letting him know it's okay to feel any emotion he feels, and our anger is our fault, not his.

We got angry because our programming said children must be obedient, and this uppity child is expressing emotions! Think about it. Our society has been at war with its children for generations. How fucked up is that?

In my and many others' case, we try to suppress emotions the adults in our life don't like. But that eventually grows to all emotions and leads to clinical depression. Rather than try to suppress, deny, or escape difficult emotions, it's far healthier to accept them or just notice them and let them move along.

In between feeling like a failed creation for feeling emotions I wasn't allowed to feel and the later depression, I spent years living in one emotion. I later learned it was fear. I thought it was anger. Either way, one emotion, and that's super fucking unhealthy. Told myself it made me strong. I prided myself on my anger. But I was lying.

I channelled all my energy into anger because it kept out other emotions, like the fear that threatened to swallow me. Like the sadness that tried to drown me. Any emotion because that'd open the door to sadness or fear, and those emotions meant weakness. So I stayed angry. Except I was really scared out of my mind and unable to cry. That led to anxiety attacks, which my brain immediately transformed into outbursts of rage.

It's weird. I knew, undoubtedly, I was at fault for everything, proving I was worthless. Yet I blamed everything on everyone else. Everybody else was to blame for everything bad that happened to me. How my crazy managed to reconcile these two opposing thoughts is quite beyond me, but I guess that's why we call it crazy, huh?

I dunno. It's hard to remember why my brain did the things it did or what I was thinking. I'm using my prefrontal cortex now, and those memories are locked away in my limbic system. I can't access them unless I'm triggered, and I can't trust my brain then, for obvious reasons. I'll tell you this for free, though: blaming other people makes it hard on your marriage. Don't do that.

Another coping mechanism my brain tried to use, or maybe defaulted to, really, was procrastination. I didn't want to deal with decision-evoking fear, so I'd procrastinate. My brain was incapable of planning, my short-term memory shot, my concentration non-existent, so I'd procrastinate. But knowing I'd hafta face my shit and make a decision kept the anxiety maxed out, so my decision-making was even more fucked, and herewegoagainmotherfucker! Stalling just kept me from concentrating and planning, which is what my brain actually needed to do. But to do that, I would've had to face my shit, and no fucking way was that gonna happen!

My attempts to help younger officers deal with or prevent stress injury? That was how I hid from my shit. Same with the first little bit of trying to help counsel inmates. Hey, fixing your shit is easy. No fucking way was I gonna deal with my own. That's way too scary.

I could hide behind altruism. I could pretend my shit was under control. If I can help others with their issues, then clearly mine are firmly under control. Except that was a lie. I'm sure you know someone just like I was. Someone who helps everyone all the time. Someone so obviously bananas you're terrified for them, but there they are, selflessly volunteering to help the mentally ill, or first responders, or veterans, or addicts. Because they're hiding.

64

I AM GRATEFUL FOR

In which our hero illustrates practising gratitude.

1. My back hurts, but I'm alive to hurt.
2. I'm cold waiting for my packages, but I can go inside.
3. My food was very delayed, but I ate because I wanted to. My appetite has returned.
4. My packages are misplaced, and I wasted an hour waiting for them, but I can afford them.
5. Coffee. Fuckin' seriously, man, coffee!
6. I'm furious, but I can regulate, but two years ago I couldn't.
7. My hip hurts, but movement will alleviate much of it, and it forces me to work out.
8. I can chat with my wife, even though she's at work.
9. It's cloudy, but I can still see plenty of blue (poetic, no?).
10. I'm not totally stable, but I'm stable enough that I can usually tell when I'm not.
11. My replacement PPCLI mug arrived from the kit shop so I can drink coffee.
12. I had nightmares about losing my family but woke up to my family.

13. My nighttime meds mess me up in the morning, but I don't lose my shit and have tantrums anymore.
14. My struggles. They've turned me into a man I'd be happy for my sons to emulate.
15. My pain. It's so good to feel anything. Numb is worse than anything.
16. After years of self-neglect and a few months of self-care, I finally benched 205 pounds for 5 × 5 and crushed the assault bike for twenty minutes.
17. My family has food to eat every day.
18. I keep finding the strength to post my shit in hopes of reaching someone in that hole.
19. My children sleep in a house, not a cardboard box.
20. Satellite radio—rock 'n' roll and country music are alive and well, if you look.
21. I remembered to turn the alarm off before letting the dogs out.
22. I've a backyard and don't have to stumble down flights of stairs so my dogs can pee.
23. I have dogs.
24. I'm finally done with that goddamn degree program and academia forever.
25. I've enough money left to complete another degree program.
26. Books.
27. Cochrane, Alberta—the foothills and the Rockies have stolen my soul.
28. I've spent years being an asocial, insecure douchebag, and yet my life is filled with people who care.
29. My wife is beautiful, inside and out, kind, intelligent, witty, healthy in body and mind.
30. My sons are beautiful, inside and out, kind, intelligent, witty, healthy in body and mind.

31. My struggles. My pain. They've gifted me with the ability to help others who're facing the same struggles and feeling the same pain.

Gratitude journal. Try it.

It works. It forces your brain to change how it thinks.

It's hard to be depressed, or angry, or lonely, or sad, or scared, or envious, or anxious when you're grateful.

65

WHY?

In which our hero explains how vulnerability equals recovery.

Why do I do this?

Why do I put my pain on the interwebs for the world to see?

Why do I risk so much?

Why do I put myself through the almost-daily anxiety?

You might think it's to help others.

You'd be wrong.

I do it for me.

I once heard LCol Dave Grossman, PhD, speak. It was on base in Petawawa, Ontario. He said a lot of important things (he also said "Hooah" a lot, but he's a Ranger).

The thing he said that resonates with me still, more and more as I heal and help others do the same, is, "Pain shared is pain divided; joy shared is joy multiplied."

It's so much easier to carry a piece of someone else's pain.

It's lighter than ours.

Letting someone else carry a piece of our pain is a win-win.

Our pain is way lighter than theirs; their pain is way lighter than ours.

It's a great trade.

Thanks for carrying a piece of mine.

Vulnerability fuels empathy.

Empathy fuels connection.

Connection heals.

My ruck gets lighter with every piece you take from me.

Share yours.

It'll help.

I promise.

66

SELF-SABOTAGE

In which our hero sheds light on the pitfalls toward recovery.

When you have to do something, do you make contingency plans, focus on your ability, and hit that shit? Me too. Usually. Now. Or are you certain you're gonna fail? Me too. But only sometimes now. It's pretty common for the mentally ill, be it depression, PTSD, or whatever, to be underachievers. When you add in attachment issues and the almost ubiquitous comorbidity of mental illnesses with substance abuse and other forms of self-sabotage, then it's no wonder why people like me clearly suck at life. I used to avoid challenge because the emotional price of failure was just too high to bear. I got over that to a large extent in the Army, but once I was medicalled out, well, that was the clearest evidence to date I was a loser: the Army kicked me out. Keep the bar low and you don't run the risk of failing, right?

If you believe you aren't good enough, that you're less than, whether through blatant verbal abuse or the subliminal teaching underpinning the reality of being Indigenous, you believe that shit. (Ah, the reality of being Indigenous in Canada: being ashamed and apologetic for existing. Get off my back, man; I didn't ask to be born!) Didn't much matter if I did accomplish something cool; I still knew I was a failure. Ugh! The nights I've lost to rumination in the wee hours, second-guessing my every decision, chewing on every failure, real or imagined, repeating every slight, real or imagined...I get so tired, sometimes, of being crazy. It's exhausting. Literally.

Here's an insight: every mistake or failure is my fault and due entirely to inherent weakness of character or innate stupidity. Period. Regardless of circumstances, it was bound to happen because I'm less than. Every success I've ever had? Well, that's just blind luck. Self-criticism at its finest, no? And to make sure I couldn't prove myself wrong, I'd find ways to not succeed. Y'all know how much I love the martial arts and combat sports... well, I don't have any accreditation to prove I know stuff about things in those fields. Y'know why? Because I wouldn't let myself progress. I'd quit classes, or stop testing, or just stop going. Self-fulfilling prophecy of failure. And y'all know I love nothing more than running around kung fu fighting!

Kids from unhealthy homes learn to hide emotions as a failed coping mechanism. We don't learn to recognize the big emotions, like anger, fear, shame. Mostly because we aren't allowed to express them, because they make our parents uncomfortable, because they weren't allowed to express them. Generations of repressed emotions...generations of parents being told if they spare the rod, they spoil the child...generations of children being seen, not heard...generations of children having to obey so their parents can feel in control...generations of parents at war with their children...

So.

Fucked.

Up.

...anyway. Some kids don't learn emotional regulation, so they try to deny their emotions; they build an emotional fortress and try not to feel at all. Problem is, they have those fucking emotions, and they'll come out, and they're going to come out at levels wildly inappropriate to the situation. Not understanding or being allowed to express emotions leads to failed coping methods and mental illness. Ask me how I know.

As a forty-five-year-old man, I had to learn how to recognize and separate emotions so I could focus on which one I was actually feeling. I had to recognize emotions blend and shift, that it's possible for me to feel more than just anger. I had to learn how to feel all my emotions, allow them out in appropriate levels at appropriate times, and tell people what I was feeling and needed. Took fucking years. But the mood swings are fewer, farther between, and less powerful now. My Window of Tolerance is wider than it has been in years.

You can do it too.

67

SOCIETAL MENTAL ILLNESS #1

In which our hero uses the legal system to illustrate how the struggle in society and our minds is the same, and how both must be addressed.

When I was at my mentally unhealthiest, I relished my use of fear over others. It kept me from confronting my own fear. I'm currently on stress leave from work. I can't work as a jail guard anymore. I cannot be a part of a failed system that relies on fear to maintain control.

I've spent the past decade using, suffering, witnessing, and constantly being on watch to prevent violence. I've no idea how many times in the past decade I've hurt a mentally ill victim of society, lost in addiction. I cannot begin to guess how many times I've watched another human be hurt.

Our society is messed up, and it messes us up. Its victims aren't just the street kids raised in poverty, neglect, abuse, addiction, and mental illness who turn into criminals. Those victims include its defenders: the peace officers who patrol its streets and its prisons.

You heard me; we're screwing up our cops. First by traumatizing them *to use* fear on our behalf, then by traumatizing them *for using* fear on our behalf. In the name of control. Because of fear. Our fear of criminals.

Why? Because it's easier. Because people want to feel safe and don't really want to look too closely at what their defenders do, whether heroic or monstrous, as long as they have Netflix and don't have to actually see the deeds that support their peace and quiet. And before you get too "holier than thou" about those defenders, I strongly suggest you read or watch a documentary about the Stanford prison experiment and see how quickly you would become a monster.

We're inflicting moral injuries on our protectors. Because of fear. Fear of stigma. The stigma they'd apply to themselves. Their fear of confronting their issues, hiding behind posturing overcompensation and puffed-up machismo. Their fear of confronting their demons. Their fear of admitting they have mental health issues and so hiding behind alcohol, religion, or toxic aggression. Their fear of self-reflection and self-improvement.

Their entire job is based on fear, and it carries into every aspect of their lives. They become so traumatized that they lose the ability to focus and their short-term memory. Their limbic systems are overwhelmed with fear. They're our victims just as much as the criminals they're required to traumatize on our behalf.

Because of our political so-called leaders' fear of us. Their fear of losing control over us. So they poison us. Our entire system is inside out and backwards. We maintained feudalism. We simply changed some names. We'd be better off if we'd kept robber barons. At least they were open and honest in their fear and extortion.

Our so-called leaders use our police to employ force and fear on their, not our, behalf, to continue their control over us. Therein lies the problem with our so-called leadership: we have none. Leadership is modelling the behaviour you wish your subordinates to exhibit. Leading the way. Being the example. (It's also a major key to parenting, FYI.) The example our leaders set is fear and punishment. Force and violence. Because they're afraid.

"Maximum security." "Law enforcement." Those phrases reek of fear. "Maintain the right." Not plural, not our rights, as in civil or human. The right. The divine right of kings? Time for an overhaul, there, I think. Words frame thoughts.

It's all counterproductive. Our mission is to make the streets safer. We do this by reducing recidivism. We do that by convincing criminals to stop being criminals, and we do that by leadership, not bullying.

I've heard many officers mock criminals for repeating behaviour and continually getting arrested, losing years of their life to imprisonment. I look at us and how we continually punish criminals when every psychology and parenting book I've ever read says punishment doesn't work and banishing children to their room counters emotional resiliency. Let me ask, would you agree with beating and locking away children who misbehave? I'm guessing not.

Violence creates violent people. Emotional and psychological healing are entirely dependent upon human connection, and it's real fucking hard to connect when you're locked behind steel doors and concrete. Psychologically proved decades ago, punishment is counterproductive.

We're the problem, you and me. We perpetuate the system because it's what we know. Judgment, punishment, hypocrisy, violence, illegality in the name of the law, immorality in the name of morality…the perpetuation of failure continues.

I think about that kid, locked in a cage, trapped in misery and mental illness and addiction and self-loathing, with nobody to give a shit, and the effect a kind word and shared pain from a male authority figure can have on him. In order for me to counsel inmates, they have to (a) trust me, and (b) believe I know what I'm talking about. I start the conversation explaining I'm an alcoholic and struggle with mental illness. Every kid I reach, that has a knock-on effect, improving his family's life and future generations. Isn't that what "corrections" is supposed to do? Or are we supposed to just continually punish failure and shitty circumstances? I have letters and cards and emails from inmates telling me they've quit drugs, gotten jobs, and have their families back in their lives.

We arrest someone with nothing. No education, no steady employment, mental health issues, addictions, horrific child-hood, no trusted circle of friends. Lock them up in a jail to ensure if they did have any supports to prevent relapse and recidivism, they don't anymore. Then kick them out on the streets. No money, no home, no job, no rehab, no therapy, no life skills, no prospects, no way to improve. The only thing we ensure they keep is mental illness and addiction.

Then we tell them they can't associate with other people with criminal records, when that's all they know, but they have to score drugs to feed their addiction, and they have to commit crime to pay for their drugs because we didn't help them. We don't "correct" criminal behaviour. We perpetuate it.

Rules don't work. Agreement works. Leadership training in the Army says so. Child psychology says so. Adult education principles say so. Common goddamn sense says so! If you tell someone what they must or mustn't do, they're probably going to tell you to go screw yourself and do what they want. You may disagree with me, but I guaran-goddamn-tee you broke rules you didn't want to obey. But if you and I agree we'll abide by an agreement, we most likely will.

We've been using fear and prisons for centuries, and crime never went away. If they worked, crime would be gone. Getting "tough on crime"? A fucking farce. We used to brand, flog, and hang criminals. Doesn't get tougher on crime than that. Yet crime is still here. I mean, shit, if it worked at all, I'd be all over it. No matter how you may feel about politics, or religion, or ideology, or whatever, facts are fucking facts, and the fact is this shit doesn't fucking work!

It doesn't fucking work!

Insanity is doing the same thing over and over and expecting a different result. If it doesn't work, and has never worked, then wouldn't a rational person try something different? Violence only creates trauma. Trauma perpetuates itself, and it's contagious. One side is afraid of violence being perpetrated on them, the other is afraid of reprisal, and the circle of fear continues.

Look in the mirror. You're the cause of crime. Just like me.

Let's find a way to help our victims, the broken people our system punishes for being broken. It isn't through a failed "justice" system run by broken souls who've been so traumatized they've no compassion or empathy left. They're broken people being used by a failed system to punish broken people.

I won't put my mind through that wringer anymore. I cannot bring that to my family, even if it never leaves my brain, anymore. It poisons them. I won't live in a numb, emotionless fog, unable to remember their names or to feed myself, broken only by irrational outbursts of rage. I won't go back to the living hell I was trapped in for so many years. My sons deserve better. I won't pass those failed coping mechanisms on to them as they were to me. The cycle ends with me.

As I've emerged from the fog of fear and loneliness and confusion, I look around, and all I see is the same fear in control of our society. Our whole damn nation is lost in the same damn fog, and we're letting it make us worse. Instead of trying to find compassion for ourselves and others, we allow fear, disguised as insecurity, disguised as envy, disguised as so many secondary emotions, to drive us apart.

We judge ourselves and therefore judge everyone else, and it fuels separation when we need connection. It has to stop. And it stops within you. Find self-compassion, be empathetic to yourself, and it spreads. Connection, empathy, vulnerability, trust... these things are just as contagious as fear. Choose which you want to feel. Choose which you want to spread.

68

STRENGTH IS VULNERABILITY

In which our hero gives examples of the importance of vulnerability.

I used to believe vulnerability meant weakness, and weakness meant a lack of manhood.

These were ideas drummed into my head from earliest childhood and constantly reinforced by culture.

I never admitted to myself that I felt fear, sorrow, stress, or any other "unmanly" emotion.

Eventually, I couldn't feel emotions at all.

My wife of twenty-three years, my first love, my love at first sight, died after a two-year battle against her eating disorder, and I was back at work a week after the funeral.

Very shortly after this, I began to have uncontrollable, irrational outbursts of sheer rage and suicidal thoughts.

Again.

By now, I had a newborn son with a new wife, and I had to confess, not only was something terribly wrong, but I had no idea what to do.

Somehow, I found the courage to admit I needed help.

It was then, upon beginning my journey to mental health, that I learned about compassion, vulnerability, and empathy.

It was through working with mental health professionals that I saw how courageous it is to be compassionate and how much strength it takes to be vulnerable.

After allowing myself to acknowledge I felt sorrow, grief, and fear, I allowed myself to also concede I felt the pain of others.

I permitted myself to feel their sorrow, their fear, their anguish, and to admit to them I felt the same emotions.

I began to actually see the inmates with whose care I was entrusted and to earnestly want to help them.

I began to speak with them, sharing my pain, so they could unburden themselves a little with me.

I began to talk with young officers about addiction, grief, PTSD, clinical depression, and anxiety so those who were suffering might find the courage to get the help I did.

I spoke with them openly and honestly, hoping they'd heed the lessons I had to learn so painfully.

And, most importantly, I began to be a dad.

Compassion and vulnerability are not things I paid much attention to, consciously, in my younger years.

I've learned so much about compassion and vulnerability, through my therapy, as a facilitator for therapy groups, and as a corrections officer.

I wonder how much better I could've been as a person had I known sooner how important it is to try to see the world through another's eyes.

69

SOCIETAL MENTAL ILLNESS #2

In which our hero uses corrections to illustrate how the fear/judgment/control struggle in society and our minds is the same.

When I began in corrections, fresh out of the Army and crazy as a shit-house rat, all inmates were subhuman, undeserving of the "luxuries" they were granted. Luxuries such as pillows, purchasing junk food, a television set in the day room, things like that.

I look back at that man. At how he relished his skill and comfort with violence and willingness to employ it. He was a bully, using violence to compensate for the fear he lived in. It makes me sadder than almost anything else that has happened to me. I feel intense shame for having let myself slide so far into madness that I gleefully violated my moral code.

So many officers overcompensate for insecurity with arrogance and blustering. They come across as bullies. It's really quite sad, when you remember they chose their career to make the world a better place. They became officers to help people. But after working in this toxic and soul-destroying occupation, they're traumatized by the job, by the violence and fear, and become as mentally ill as the criminals they've more in common with than the citizenry they protect.

The truly sad part is this becomes their full-time persona. It's why so many are divorced, with children who won't return their phone calls and have morbid obesity and substance abuse issues. Hiding from reality with booze or religion, anything to prevent independent thought. That would mean confronting the reality that they're ill. Then they'd have to accept they need help and... well, can't do that shit. That means weakness. Self-judgment applied as fiercely as they judge the broken souls they're responsible for arresting or incarcerating. These are all classic textbook trauma responses.

Now, after having learned to be compassionate with myself as I progressed through therapy to treat my own mental illness...well, I see inmates differently. I've learned to see the humans in those coveralls. I've worked very hard to earn the trust of inmates so I can pass along the lessons I've learned from my battles to defeat my demons. By sharing openly with inmates, I've been able to guide many of them toward addiction treatment, re-establishing connections with loved ones they've pushed away, and putting serious effort into rehabilitation.

I see the results when inmates get the help and tools to deal with their issues. I see what happens when addicts get treatment, the mentally ill get therapy and medication, and homeless people are given a safe place to stay. I see what happens when inmates receive lessons in childcare and anger management and develop job skills. What happens is I see them less.

And I see what happens to the ones who don't get any of this (or choose not to take advantage of it). I see them more. They get more addicted and involved in more serious crimes until they get locked up forever or die in a gutter.

I just had a conversation with an inmate I hadn't seen in years. He took the advice I gave him and the treatment options that were available. He's been sober for six years. He's got a job and a place to live. He's pleading guilty to his remaining charges to finish any and all time required so he can start over without anything owed to the Crown. Free man, clean slate.

I showed a homeless addicted man how to utilize the system to get help from the agencies in place dedicated to that. He was on the phone, calling one of those agencies, when I left him. He was so happy, thinking he could break the cycle.

I had a talk with a young girl in our observation wing a while ago. She was on suicide watch. She told me about her horrific childhood, about her father letting his dealers use her pre-pubescent body to pay for his fix, about her sister's death from an overdose, and more I won't inflict on you. We talked, addict to addict. Two people who understand trauma. Two people who've wanted to kill themselves to end the pain. Two people dealing with mental illness. She was cleared from suicide watch after that.

Today, she told me her plan to get treatment upon winning her case (which seems likely) and go to therapy to deal with her shit, and her desire to get her children back and learn how to be a mom. Two days ago, I was crying for her pain (and I had to work hard not to vomit, to be honest). Today, I teared up because her face shone. All she needed was someone to share pain with. Now she's dead set on rehabilitating herself.

Now I want to pass along these lessons I've learned about the injustice inherent in the justice system. Maybe our society will stop punishing the poor for being poor, and punishing the addicted for being addicts, and punishing the Indigenous for being Indigenous, and punishing the traumatized and mentally ill for being traumatized and mentally ill.

Be grateful you're able to pretend these people don't exist. That they get swept up like the human detritus they are and hidden from your view. I see them. I hear them. I hear the traumas inflicted on them by their parents: beatings, neglect, starvation, sexual abuse, awfulness piled on trauma added to horror. Do they have any options, really? Raised in poverty and surrounded by criminality and addiction, what're you going to become? You can't do well academically or athletically because no money is spent on you to develop academically and athletically. You don't know anything other than hopelessness.

Our legal system isn't designed to stop crime or help its victims. It's designed to ensure the elite remain the elite. It's designed to ensure the screwed-over remain screwed-over. We still swear allegiance to the Crown. The definition of *allegiance* is "loyalty or commitment of a subordinate to a superior" according to Oxford. We owe vassalage to Parliament, and crimes are actions that offend the honour of the Crown. Not actions that affect humans in a negative way, acts against the Crown. Insubordination. Disloyalty.

There is no regard for the humans involved, on either side. The person who has offended the dignity of the Crown must be punished. Right now, in some courthouse, people are gathering to discuss what punishment should be given to a man for insulting the honour of a monarch who has no fucking idea her honour was slighted rather than trying to heal a broken man who'll therefore continue to commit crimes and trying to heal the victim who'll never recover.

Locks only keep out honest men. Laws only work on the law-abiding. I learned as a child laws are something to find a way around. Laws are for rich people. So I obeyed rules enforced by someone bigger and stronger than me. When they were around. Compliance versus cooperation. Both involve a relationship, but only one is mutually rewarding. Mutually rewarding agreements mean both parties will stick to them.

Trying to survive the streets is exactly like trying to survive in the bush. It takes every ounce of effort and wit. You've no time to spend on anything other than finding food and shelter from the elements and predators. Then, because your life is a shower of shit, you hide from reality in drugs. And then you gotta hide from the cops who're hired to hunt you down instead of being allowed to focus on truly evil people. All that cash wasted chasing people who'd fucking jump at the chance to stop living the way they live.

The Canadian "justice" system is endemic with fear, and fear breeds violence. I won't be a party to othering, the same mentality that created the SS, the KGB, and Reserves. I refuse to be a weapon anymore. I refuse to live in or create fear. Fear prevents communication. Fear prevents connection.

Don't allow fear to rule you. Don't allow others to use fear to rule you. Fear is the enemy. Fear is the way to madness. Connection, compassion, vulnerability…these things have healed my broken mind and can heal our broken society. Trust, honesty, empathy…start displaying these things to yourself and they'll just sorta naturally start leaking out to the world and, fuck me, does the world need that shit right now!

70

INDIGENEITY

In which our hero uses race to illustrate mental illness factors such as judgment and intergenerational trauma.

First, this isn't attacking anybody. If it makes you angry, ask yourself why. Anger isn't going to help, and we're just gonna dance the same dance. Second, it isn't "Poor me, I'm so hard done by; I'm a helpless victim." I'm not lookin' to guilt-trip you or make you feel shitty. I know you're not racist, or you wouldn't be reading this. Besides, when someone is genuinely apologetic and you keep rubbing their nose in it, they stop being apologetic. I'm just pointing out shit I've lived. Might give you a new perspective. Might not.

I know race doesn't define you unless you let it. I also know life is harder when you look different. I know this. I have family that look more Indigenous than others. I've seen how the Canadian majority interacts with them. I got beat up by white kids because my mom looked Indigenous, and by Indigenous kids because my dad looked white. I learned people are all shitty, no matter their colour, and I learned how to fight.

As an Indigenous man with Caucasian skin, I've found myself in the unenviable position of hearing the Canadian majority talk about the Indigenous in an…unfiltered…manner. When "they" believe "they" are "alone," if you will. I usually found myself enraged; most often by the leftist intelligentsia, the social justice warriors who protest on my family's behalf but would never invite my relations into their homes. The smarmy, self-congratulatory land recognition drives me bananas. "We recognize we are on the traditional lands of…" Great. Y'ain't givin' it back, though, is ya? Social justice warriors make me crazy with their hypocrisy. Hey! You! The woke social justice warrior! You're every bit as racist, paternalistic, and full of shit as your colonist ancestors, with their Great White Father. My slanty eyes and high cheekbones don't mean I'm stupid, okay? I don't need you to take care of me. I need you to get the fuck out of my way.

Anyway…about how Indigeneity ties into mental illness at the individual and communal level…

I hate me. Can you understand that? Self-loathing is the source of all my shit because it started in earliest childhood. I didn't develop emotional resiliency sufficient to deal with later traumatic events. Doesn't fuckin' matter what I accomplish. Doesn't matter how much others may respect my achievements. Doesn't matter what medals and commendations hang on my wall. I hate me, in part, because I was taught all my life, both overtly and subliminally, I am not as good as, lesser than. Because my Indigenous ancestors walked here twenty-some thousand years before my white ancestors sailed here. Because I'm First Nations. Because I exist.

Not as good as. Lesser than.

I was raised in a Metis family burdened with shame. Indigenous, by definition in Canada, is "lesser than. Not as good as. I was taught I'm Metis, and unconsciously taught not to talk about that with non-family. I was subconsciously taught to be ashamed of existing because we're lesser than. Out of shame. (Y'see, shame and guilt are different. Guilt = I did a bad thing. Shame = I'm a bad person. Shame destroys your soul. Shame isn't ours to carry. It gets put on us by others, through judgment.) Shame is the lot of the Indigenous. Shame for existing.

Not as good as. Lesser than.

The First Nations have been taught to be ashamed of existing for generations. For decades, we weren't allowed to leave the Reserves. Banished from the rest of the world. Except the children, who were taken to residential schools so they could be tortured and raped and taught to be ashamed of their ancestry. Ashamed of existing.

Not as good as. Lesser than.

This idea I had as a child, where I'm not as good as my peers, is, in fact, a psychological risk factor that increased the odds of my having mental health and addiction issues later in life. Boy, did it work. I didn't live in poverty and squalor; my parents worked hard, and we had food. That there wasn't lots of money led me to thievery (I stole books). I narrowly evaded being raped on three separate occasions before and during puberty. I started abusing booze and tobacco so early, I can't recall how old I was.

Not as good as. Lesser than.

Coulda been so much worse. I always had potable drinking water. Not every Indigenous child does. I had food and a roof. My parents didn't beat or rape or sell me. This is all mild compared to life on the "Rez" or for Indigenous people in urban centres. For centuries, we've been told we're not as good as. Tell a child they're no good, what happens to their self-esteem? What happens to a child with low self-esteem? Now amplify that by a million for 150 years.

Not as good as. Lesser than.

It doesn't stop. It's everywhere. It's subliminal and programmed into the Canadian zeitgeist. Even people who "aren't racist" are racist. As an Indigenous man with white skin (well, technically my skin is multicoloured, with my tats), I've heard people who aren't racist say racist shit, my father and wives included. My wives were/are both very white (nearly translucent, in fact). And, clearly, they've no problem with Indigenous people. After all, both knowingly married one. Dennette made two. Pretty not-racist, no? Both of them used to say racist crap until I could show them they'd been taught myths all their lives.

Not as good as. Lesser than.

Kids used to play cowboys and Indians, copying what they saw on TV and the movies. Indians were always the bad guy. Except Tonto. He was just a poorly spoken semi-idiot who tagged along with the Lone Ranger. Now he's a lunatic played by Johnny Depp, a white actor with a stuffed bird on his head. *Plus ça change, plus c'est la même chose.*

Not as good as. Lesser than.

Can you name any place in Canada where entire communities of whites have lived for decades without clean drinking water because they can't go anywhere else? Look into how many Reserves in Canada have lived that way for twenty years. If your family members go missing, can you be certain the police will look for them? I can't. I've stunningly beautiful nieces and cousins. I can't be sure they'll be looked for if they disappear. Canada kills Indigenous girls, especially beautiful ones.

Not as good as. Lesser than.

There's a bar in a town I lived in for a while. It has a steel railing that runs across the building. If you're native, you don't cross that line unless you're looking for a beating. My first father-in-law explained I was okay to date his daughter because I looked white and I worked, so I wasn't "really Indian" to him. I feel intense shame every day because I'm so grateful my sons don't look native. Because their lives will be easier and safer.

Not as good as. Lesser than.

Entire generations of academics seem to be missing something I learned from therapy. The First Nations are adrift in a crisis of identity loss, depression, anxiety, addiction, and PTSD. From believing we were put here with responsibilities from the Creator to care for the land upon which he placed us, to having land and responsibilities both taken away by treachery. Where the First Nations have been demanding our responsibilities be returned, Canadian mythology says we're looking for a free ride. The lazy, dumb, drunken Indian stereotype became entrenched in the Canadian zeitgeist as a means to justify othering and genocide.

Not as good as. Lesser than.

I saw a quote attributed to Senator Murray Sinclair: "Reconciliation will never be achieved so long as one side sees it as a recognition of rights, and the other side sees it as an act of benevolence." It's a race between reconciliation and annihilation. It's hard to reconcile when our children die in droves. Die from diseases other communities don't fear, from malnutrition, from mass suicide, from murder, from abuse and neglect. Die from being Indigenous. It took two hundred years to get here; the "Rez" may achieve its aim of genocide in another two hundred.

Not as good as. Lesser than.

(Oh, and critical race theory is bullshit. You can't get rid of racism by promoting racism, so...yeah. Critical race theory is judgment and othering. You can't create a culture of diversity, inclusivity, and tolerance by preaching judgment and othering.)

I dunno...maybe if both sides can put aside the recriminations, guilt, history, shame, and fear, come together from a place of curiosity rather than presumption, display vulnerability and expect trust, give empathy and expect connection...maybe we can stop the genocide before it becomes *fait accompli*. Maybe we can heal all of the peoples of this land. Maybe if we both work on our shit and help the other with their shit, we can drop this victim/oppressor stuff and learn from history instead of continuing to relive it.

It works in individual therapy.

It works in group therapy.

It works in healing circles.

Why wouldn't it work here?

I'll work on my trauma; you work on your guilt; let's both drop our shame.

Seems worth trying to me.

71

JUDGMENT #1

In which our hero addresses the justice system as an allegory to discuss judgment and mental illness.

I don't know how much actual sense this is going to make, as it exploded into my brain and onto my screen from weeks of sleepless, feverish disgust at the world around me and years of therapy to understand my struggles with insanity. Humans really are the shittiest of the peoples. Furred people are just better.

We pretend we're logical and rational, but really, we're just primates, roaring like gorillas or screeching like spider monkeys. Emotionally speaking, we're no different from the *Homo sapiens* that first bitched and moaned their way across what's now the Middle East. Fear rules us. We either accept the tribes we're born into or choose others, but we're all about judging and othering. Out of fear. It's tit-for-tat othering. I've been othered and so I other in return. As ye have judged, so shall ye be judged. An eye for an eye. No wonder why we're all fuckin' blind.

We call criminals "evil." Can you think of a more judgmental term? There's nothing worse than that word, is there? Traumatized children in adult bodies trying to survive as best they know how. We call them "evil." Unless, of course, a judge (hmmm… judge…ment) declares them to be so mentally ill they aren't responsible for their actions. If a judge says they're insane, we don't call them "evil" and judge them; we call them "crazy" and pity them. We pretend mental illness is a light switch: on, off. Sane. Insane. Incorrect. It's a dimmer switch with uncountably different shades. But the poor are just fucking lazy, and addicts are just weak of character, right?

Are criminals lazy and bad people, or were they born and trapped in poverty and trauma by shitty circumstance? No matter how far our so-called cultural elites like to pretend they've "progressed" with their bullshit social sciences and behavioural studies, they, and therefore we, still judge every-fucking-body all the fucking time. Period. And, hey, it's always negative, right? Either because judging others negatively helps us ignore how shitty our own lives are or because it's just fun to be mean. (Which is why our repulsive social justice warrior movement and cancel culture are so vile. Pure judgment from anonymity, so cruelty knows no bounds.) Or, for those of us with mental illness, diagnosed or not, it's just how our brains work, except we're judging ourselves and finding ourselves lacking. So, because we judge everybody all the time, we still pass laws based on judgment, without learning from yesterday to improve tomorrow.

Trying to strike a balance between emotions and logic might be impossible (I haven't figured out how yet, and I've been at it for five years), but we have to try. Our hearts say everything has to be fair, to be just. Our heads say it ain't possible, because of programming from tribalism. (Some idiots try to use Marxism to answer the call of the heart, but that shit don't work. It can't. It's based on violence and judgment.) I believe it's possible, though, to be just. Our heads gotta serve our hearts. But we gotta stop doing what we've always done, 'cuz we'll just keep gettin' what we've always got.

Leftists and right-wingers disagreeing over justice is as stupid as the proverbial blind men arguing over an elephant's appearance. If they'd stop yelling long enough to listen to each other, we could the find root causes of injustice and a goddamn solution. To get to a just society, we hafta grip our fear-controlled, troglodyte tribal minds and stop pointing fingers. We need to get past judgment and use our heads. We need to listen to psychologists and anthropologists (y'know, actual scientists who want to help people?) and listen to each other without trying to blame anybody. Just listen with curiosity and empathy.

What's the saying? Judge the sin, not the sinner? Too often, we judge somebody's behaviour without asking, "Why did they do that?" What're the specific life experiences, thought patterns, and emotional states that brought that person to do that thing at that time? If we don't try to factor all that in, all we can do is judge based on a snapshot in time. Life ain't a snapshot. Each of our lives is a movie, and we all walk onto other people's movie sets at different parts of the movie.

All humans need to feel seen, heard, and understood. All humans want to be treated with respect, so do it. Lower your ego and you lower your fear. Lower your fear and you lower your judgment. Try to see through that person's eyes to understand how they got there and made the choices they did. You both see the situation, sure, but you both see it differently. If we try to decode the situation based on our values, we take a snapshot and frame it in our experiences and beliefs.

When we judge, we're looking through our perception of that person's personality, not the actual situation or their perception of it. We're unfair if we assume our beliefs about someone else's character are fact, rather than looking impartially at the situation, especially if our beliefs about that person are wrong. We're unfair and so unjust. We hafta look at their actions, consider their reasons, and not let our biases tell us that person is just bad. Judge the sin, not the sinner.

The more I learn about anything, the less certain I am about everything. I miss being twenty-three. I knew everything then, and I was dead certain about all of it. Now I can't be certain I'm wearing pants half the fucking time, let alone be certain I know someone else's motives for doing anything. We hafta remember shit will probably pop up later that may change our minds about that person's actions, morals, and character. If we've already judged, we can't leave our minds open to new facts. Judgment, not justice, is absolute.

Judgment is fear. Fear is ignorance. Fear is division and separation, which fuels ignorance, which fuels fear. It's a vicious circle of ugly. It only ends when we try to be open and trusting. When we give vulnerability a chance. When we approach a person or situation with curiosity and courage.

My disgust at what I've seen in academia and the revulsion I experience the rare times I accidentally see, hear, or read any of the mainstream media have driven me to a state of depression I haven't experienced in years. I cannot sleep without medical assistance. I'm angry all day, every day, and that isn't acceptable, as it leaks out into my family's life. Perhaps this message will function as a journal of sorts, allowing me to vent my spleen at the tyranny I see created by postmodernism, fueled by the media and the universities.

I prefer to just go with the incredible wisdom I learned in kindergarten: treat everyone like you want to be treated. If Seneca, Confucius, Gautama Buddha, and Jesus of Nazareth all agree on something, it's probably a good idea. They were all pretty smart cats. Do with this as you will, my friend.

72

JUDGMENT #2

In which our hero addresses a root cause of the increasing prevalence of mental illness today.

Why is everything so fucked up right now? Why is our culture revolving around division, hate, judgment, and othering? Why are rates of mental illness skyrocketing? Because for decades now, the universities have been promoting either outright Marxism or neo-Marxism under the name postmodernism. By definition, Marxism is othering, division, judgment, and hate. Our post-secondary institutions indoctrinate our children with this vileness, paid for with our goddamn tax dollars. Generations of teachers have been indoctrinated, down to our kindergartens.

I know, I know. I'm always telling y'all to strive for compassion and empathy. Seek to understand before being understood. Come from a place of curiosity. I still stand by that, but I cannot stomach the vile, unscientific ideology that is Marxism. The revulsion I feel watching my classmates swallow this propaganda poisons my mind. And why wouldn't they? They get graded on swallowing and regurgitating this shit, and thus the psychological manipulation continues.

No, this isn't a conspiracy theory. A few years back, around 2015 or '16, something like 25 percent of university professors in the social sciences and humanities proudly declared themselves Marxists. If 25 percent totally endorse this evil, and it's still taught, then we have to assume there isn't 75 percent arguing against it. We have to assume there is an equally large percentage who support it. So, if that is one useful idiot or fellow traveller for every zealot, we're looking at around 50 percent. But even at 50 percent, there'd be some resistance to it. No, the only assumption we can make is at least 75 percent of professors in the social sciences and humanities are Marxists. Decades of brainwashing in an echo chamber will do that.

Marxism led to around 100 million murders, the imprisonment of tens of millions, the oppression of hundreds of millions, and the sponsorship of decades of international terrorism. Marxists pretend Marxism was hijacked by tyrants, but a fucking century of failure proves the idea was just insane. A century of failure would lead any scientist to call the experiment a total failure. Only an idiot would refuse to accept the evidence. But Marxism is an ideology, and ideologues cannot see reason any more than religious fanatics.

Marxist apologists spew bullshit like "Marxism is different than Communism." Nope. Karl Marx called it *The Communist Manifesto*. It's in the fucking name! Marx preached dictatorship using "despotic inroads"; there were "no excesses" in revolution, and "hated individuals" should be "murdered by popular revenge." Those're his own fucking words! Marx's endorsement of genocide: "There is only one way in which the murderous death agonies of the old society and the bloody birth throes of the new society can be shortened, simplified and concentrated, and that way is revolutionary terror." Sounds like the current wokeness / cancel culture, doesn't it?

Marx said democracy was "vulgar," families were "disgusting," and human rights were "bourgeois freedom." No democracy, no human rights, and no parental love. I understand, however, he stuck to his guns and abandoned a child he fathered on Friedrich Engels's servant. Let's let that sink in, shall we? He sponged off Engels all his life. Engels had servants. These two lived in wealth, yet demanded the wealthy be murdered. Not unlike university professors pushing Marxism while collecting paycheques roughly double my own. Well, some animals are more equal than others.

And that's my biggest gripe with Marxism: it's so fucking juvenile. Rich people whining they don't have enough and it's someone else's fault. Complaining about how unfair Mommy and Daddy are.

Marxism isn't only a proven failure; it's bloody evil! His followers have all been equally evil...Joseph Stalin, Mao Zedong, Pol Pot...Che Guevara! The guy morons wear on their T-shirt to show how woke they are? The son of a rich man demanding rich men be murdered. Calling Dr. Freud? He used to put homosexual people in front of firing squads to be murdered for the "crime" of being born gay! Murdering innocent people because of their DNA.

The thought of anyone hating any of my gay friends makes me

furious and sad. The idea of anyone trying to physically harm any of my gay friends, for hate, stokes a murderous rage in me. I cannot even begin to state how repugnant it is that this repulsive and evil philosophy is taught anywhere.

Postmodernism is a continuation of Marxism and has created this tyrannical wokeness / cancel culture that promotes hate and division. Postmodernism, like Marxism, is obsessed with power. Power is just another word for control, and people most obsessed with control are most afraid. You see it all the time with the mentally ill; the more lost we become in our illness, the harder we strive to control everything in our lives, especially the people. Bullies want control, and bullies are all inherently cowards.

Postmodernists says there is no Good or Truth, and everything is subjective, to get rid of the ideals our society is built upon. Like Liberty or Justice. By their own standards, if nothing is true, then why the fuck should I listen to them? They aren't speaking truth! According to postmodernists, nobody can be wrong, so nobody can be right. So, they ain't right. In the head. If there're no absolute truths, then scientifically established facts, like fucking gravity, can't work. And yet they do.

It's a spoiled teenager mad at their parents' rules while enjoying the best life possible, thanks to their parents. I dunno, classical liberal thought brought us to the best society that has existed to date. Denying that for postmodernism is leaving your dance partner for someone dressed flashier, only to find they can't dance. And have no personality. And bad breath. We've had centuries of examples that hating never leads to anything good.

Blaming someone else for your misery is insanity. Your misery is a result of your emotional choices. Nobody can fix that shit for you, only you. Blame is judgment. Judgment drives division and isolation. Division and isolation are insanity.

That's why everything is so fucked up. That's why our entire culture revolves around division and hate and judgment and othering. That's why rates of mental illness are skyrocketing.

Marx and Michel Foucault were bad men, and their legacy is exactly that: do bad things. Yeah, Foucault, the hero of the postmodernists, signed a petition demanding pedophilia be legalized. And universities teach this creature's nonsense without the decency of a whispered "trigger warning." As a child who narrowly escaped being raped three times, I cannot begin to describe how fucking grotesque it is that the lies of a goddamn pedophile are being taught. I'm extremely uncomfortable bathing my two sons because of pedophiles, and academe praises a pedophile.

Empathy, connection, and compassion…that's the shit we need right now, as individuals and a culture. Show compassion to yourself. If you don't, you can't be compassionate to others. I learned that shit the hard way. Wokeness / cancel culture is hate disguised as compassion, just as Marxism is tyranny disguised as egalitarianism, and postmodernism is the bridge of hate between them. It's emotionally dysregulated children of all ages hating a person on behalf of a third person. Compassion works better.

Empathy, connection, and compassion. They're harder than hate and judgment, the battle cry of wokeness / cancel culture. Empathy means trying to see the world through the lens of another person. Trying to see, hear, and understand by trying to put oneself in that person's place. Trying to learn how their life brought them to this place and time and how we can make their life less hellish. Help those you can, and your life becomes less hellish.

I despise organized religion but respect Gautama Buddha and Jesus of Nazareth. They walked the earth trying to do good. The Mahatma and Dr. Martin Luther King Jr. had failings as men, because they were men, but they tried to do good and achieved much. Their legacy shines forever. I know who I'd rather hang out with. What a dinner conversation that would be, huh?

73

CONFLICT

In which our hero addresses conflict, isolation, and their connection to mental illness.

Gautama Buddha said human suffering is caused by desire. I have to respectfully disagree. Human suffering is caused by fear. Fear of insecurity. Fear of judgment. Fear of the unknown. Fear of the new. Fear of change. Bear with me; it'll make sense in a bit.

All living things, including humans, seek homeostasis, not happiness. Unconsciously, we often prefer suffering horribly to improving our situation because that's change. Confronting the unknown is terrifying. So we suffer. This is the life of the addict. I know; I'm an alcoholic. I suffered with PTSD, depression, anxiety, and other shit for decades before seeking help. Because misery was comfortable. Unpleasant, but comfortable. Normal. Homeostasis.

My misery (I don't know how the brain did this) was everybody else's fault, but I was totally at fault because I'm worthless. No way was I gonna face that shit, so it was everybody else's fault. And around and around we go.

Once I stopped blaming external factors and worked on rewording my self-narrative, I found periods of calm and joy. If we look inwards, we see how all our suffering is brought on by our own fucking fears. Social media, television, magazines, movies, pop music...all these things glorify materialism and a bullshit idea of what life is. They drive separation, and we suffer as a species because of it. Messed up, huh? Think about it, though, and you'll agree.

Society glorifies the rugged individual. The tough-guy loner. I've seen every John Wayne cowboy movie at least a dozen times. They're all wrong, emotionally speaking. Look inward and reach outward to heal. Look inward to see what your brain is doing. Then reach out for the social acceptance we need. We heal from connection. Connection to ourselves and other humans. Stop looking outward for happiness. It ain't out there. Your misery is inside. So is your happiness.

Look inward to find your better life. You can't find contentment outside, man; it's an emotion. It's in your head, along with insecurity, fear, self-loathing, and other shit you don't need. Stop comparing yourself to other people. Compare you to you. Are you doing better today than yesterday? No? Are you trying? Let go of the bullshit society is trying to make you believe, and fix the things you can control. That's pretty much just you. I'd argue all of history's philosophers and modern psychology preach the same message. Maybe we oughta listen?

Right...conflict. Conflict begins with us. Conflict starts in our brain, in our limbic system. Everything we perceive first gets scanned by the limbic system for threats. Conflict is a common result. We read body language, tone, their words, and our brain processes it. But it does it through our previous experiences, and that can change everything. Two people can understand the same situation completely differently. And one of them can feel threatened.

If we feel threatened in any way, whether a physical threat to our safety like a bear, or an emotional threat to social status or beliefs, the amygdala launches us into fight or flight. We're triggered and react emotionally, with disastrous consequences if our reaction is inappropriate to the situation. If we've suffered trauma, that's likely. The traumatized mind sees a bear every-fucking-where. Our brains are in hypervigilance mode, and we're always ready to fight or run.

Traumatized or not, we need to get out of our own way. We gotta settle our inner conflict, calm ourselves down, or we can't reach resolution with someone else. How can we be at peace with someone else if we're fighting ourselves? To resolve any outer form of conflict, we gotta try to put our personal shit aside. If we can pull this off, we can usually use communication tools and find resolution with somebody else.

Seek connection through vulnerability and empathy. That's how we fix shit. As I've grown more compassionate with myself and found the strength to be vulnerable, I've become more empathetic with others. As I do, my suffering ebbs away. The solution to life's shittiness is to focus on yourself, figure out why you're dissatisfied, take a sec to get your shit together, then find the strength to be vulnerable and empathetic. That shit is the solution to the world's problems. By understanding your own insecurities, you change how you see the world. If everybody could push their insecurity aside and put the well-being of others before their own, the world would heal overnight. Quash our inner conflict and we'd quash most outer conflict.

74

UNDER YOUR THUMB

In which our hero illustrates the importance of responsibility in battling mental illness.

When I was lost in depression, I wouldn't try to better my circumstances and blamed the world for my misery. I tried absolutely nothing, and I was quickly all out of ideas. All living creatures seek homeostasis. This same idea applies to mental illness.

We take comfort in the devil we know. Add in childhood programming, or wonky brain wiring, or trauma, and you can end up with a recipe for emotional disaster. Humans want to be comfortable, and we adapt real fucking well to any environment. Once we've adapted, we'd rather be utterly miserable in the comfortable known than risk discomfort by improving our situation with the scary unknown.

It's part of why I wouldn't seek help. Don't do what I did. Own your shit. Take accountability for your life. Accept responsibility for your own betterment.

Ignorance breeds fear. Learn. Knowledge dispels ignorance. The "for Dummies" books contain pretty much everything you could want to learn about every-fucking-thing under the sun. Google Scholar is your friend.

You're your own point man. Be alert; be aware. You probably don't need to watch for IEDs, but a kid on a skateboard can be almost as dangerous. Active shooters? Not real high on my list of worries. Some moron asshole texting and driving while high? Legit and valid concern.

You're your own bodyguard. Train your body and your mind to defend yourself. Speed and aggression will most often carry the day, if you decide to be aggressive enough, swiftly enough. Training and physical fitness are pretty helpful too.

You're your own paramedic. Practise your first aid skills; get as in-depth instruction as you can. Stock more than one first aid kit, and keep your medicine cabinet full; keep the tools you need to preserve and protect your health, and that of others handy.

You're your own lawyer. Know the law; more important, know the laws that protect your rights. That said, remember, the one who defends himself in court has a fool for a client.

You're your own financial advisor. Educate yourself on how to grow your income, reduce your expenditures, and preserve your property. Seek an accountant who thinks beating the system is fun and a stockbroker who works on a percentage of your profit, not a salary.

You cannot be your own psychologist. You can't see what you

can't see. Your shit gets in the way. You need someone else to tell you what your brain is trying to do to you and how to stop it.

Don't let fear keep you from seeking an expert. Nobody can specialize in everything. Learn all you can about all you encounter, but recognize your limitations. Then seek to surpass them. Don't let fear keep you from learning and growing. The more you learn, the less you fear, and the more you'll grow.

Change is hard.

Change is scary.

Change stays difficult and frightening. Until it doesn't and isn't. That's when you know you've changed.

Change is necessary.

Change is growth.

Whether you've total control over your circumstances (unlikely) or not, you do have total control over how you choose to perceive them and whether you choose to accept them as they are. You've the option to choose to better yourself. You can make the choice to better your circumstances.

Ultimately, since perception is reality, you do have total control over your situation because you can control how you want to see it.

75

PTSD #1

In which our hero explains post-traumatic stress disorder.

Let's talk about PTSD a bit, shall we? Lotta bullshit out there about it, mostly promulgated by Hollywood. First, we all picture PTSD as being caused by a major, horrible event. Well, that happens, sure, but there's another type. I had a regimental sergeant major look at me once and say, "Yeah, it's cumulative," in reference to another soldier's trauma and stress. He was a smart man, the ol' RSM. Another smart man described it to me this way (and I'm wildly paraphrasing here, but the gist is correct):

Imagine you're walking along a trail in the woods. You got your pack on; sun's shining; life is good…bang! You walk into a tree and bust your nose. Then you fall off the trail and smash yourself up falling down the mountain. That's the one kind of PTSD.

The other is like this: imagine you're walking along a trail in the woods. You got your pack on, sun's shining, life is good… ow! You stub your toe on a rock on the trail. Now, for some odd reason, your next instinct is to pick that rock up and stuff it into your backpack. You walk on a couple miles and stub your toe again. Same damn toe too! Now, again, you pick that rock up and stuff it into your backpack. And so it goes; every few miles, you stub your same damn toe, pick that rock up, and stuff it into your backpack. After a while, that toe is so painful you can barely hobble, and the weight on your back is so heavy, you just…thump! Fall flat on your face and bust your nose. Then you fall off the trail and smash yourself up falling down the mountain.

Both times a nose got broken and someone left the path in a pretty awful way, but the second time took a lot longer to get there. Both times, life got real bad afterwards. I ain't saying one is worse than the other or any silly shit like that. Pain is pain. It just sucks all over. But it's important you realize this shit is way more complicated than most folks want to accept. People want easy. Mental illness isn't easy. Trauma isn't easy. Stress overload isn't easy. When you add in things like failed coping mechanisms and insecure attachment issues and reverse emotional resiliency programming with children…yeah, it ain't fucking easy.

Oh, but wait! There's more! So, PTSD isn't necessarily a result of a traumatic event at all! Another way to fuck up a person is by being a dick. Lemme 'splain. We've all seen the movie or TV show where the young rookie and a grizzled veteran survive a firefight. Kid's all freaked out and tries to turn to the vet for support, and the vet goes, "Suck it up, princess!" Okay, kid might very well have been just fine, but now he's all kinds of messed up.

See, teaching kids they aren't allowed to experience emotions (boys can't cry because it's weakness; girls can't be angry because it's unladylike) turns kids into walking piles of shame. How can a child not experience emotions? They're being told they aren't allowed to do that, but they can't stop doing it. So, clearly, they're flawed as humans and there's something fundamentally wrong with them, and whoooo boy! Congratulations, moron, you've just set that kid up perfectly for mental illness. But I digress.

PTSD is a normal reaction to an abnormal event. Telling a human they aren't allowed to be freaked out by a situation that is eminently freak-out-able sets them up for shame. Telling a rookie they can't be scared or have any other reasonable emotional reaction just tells them they're flawed as humans and therefore weak! Now they can't talk about the thing they most need to talk about. And the shame sets in. *Et voila!* PTSD.

Saddest part of it all is that grizzled old John Wayney, Clint Eastwoody vet is almost certainly so PTSDed-out, he can't function in society without booze. And he's contagious because he infected that rookie, who'll now devote themselves to never allowing anyone to ever know they've normal human reactions to abnormal events. And so the cycle continues. Stigma and shame. Mental illness and substance abuse.

So, what can we do about it? Well, we give other humans the freedom to experience and express the whole range of emotions they actually feel, for one. Crazy, huh?

"Oh, what's that, little boy? You're sad and want to cry? Well, shit, son, lemme just sit down and cry right with you. After, you can tell me what we're crying about."

"Hey, little girl, you're angry? Well, you let 'er rip! Get mad and get loud! Cuss and holler. When you run out of cuss words, I'll give you a few. I know lots."

"What's going on, rookie? That shit was nine kinds of fucked up, huh? I dunno about you, but I was so scared, I'd have wet my pants if I hadn't been totally dehydrated from sweating so much. Man, that was messed up. Glad you're okay, kid."

Now, what about the folks who've already had their emotions crushed by some asshole somewhere? Well, we need to give them the thing all humans need as much as food or oxygen: to feel seen, heard, and understood. We sit our asses down and listen to them, suspending judgment and striving for curious empathy. When they're done telling their story, we tell them, honestly and displaying vulnerability, how their story made us feel. We let them know their emotions, then and now, are totally acceptable and we validate them. We give them the positive social response they needed then, whether it was last week or in World War II.

We do this crazy thing where we love them and be kind to them. Weird, huh?

76

TO MY SONS #18

In which our hero explains how society passes on mental illness and how to save the next generation.

Dadding is hard. I've no idea if I'm doing it right, but I'm always convinced I'm screwing it up. Everything makes me believe I've emotionally scarred you and set you up for emotional failure. I've been told I'm wrong, but that's the depressed mind: we look for the negative and can always find evidence to fulfill our prophecies of doom. But that wasn't what I wanted to talk about with you today.

My job is to prepare you for the world. I have to find the balance between pushing you and holding you back, giving you freedom and sheltering you from harm. I can't ever say "Never..." I have to say things like "Not yet." I have to support and empower you. Sometimes that means cajoling, encouraging, or barking orders. And it's really fucking hard to figure out when to do what. It's also really hard to explain "why" or "why not" to a five- and three-year-old. I forget that you forget. I can't remember you might not recall something in five minutes. It's super frustrating, I know. I'm sorry. I'm trying, boys.

I want to shelter you from all of life's ills, including making decisions. I tell myself it's love. It's fear of not having control. (Hi! My name's Sheridan, and I'm a helicopter mom. Try to imagine how embarrassing it is to say that!) So I have to give you decision-making power. I never learned emotional regulation. I didn't know how to deal with my emotions, so I didn't know how to deal with your anger, sadness, fear, or any fucking emotion at all. At least I didn't do stupid shit like send you to your room to "calm down" more than once.

That just subliminally tells the kid they're inherently flawed because they have emotions. They can't tell their parents are emotionally illiterate and too fucking stupid to read a parenting book, so they assume their parents are mad at them for having normal, healthy emotions. The cycle of emotional failure continues, and the rates of mental illness increase.

Y'see, boys, the whole mentality is incorrect. Like so much in this fucked-up culture. The phrases "raising children" and "child rearing," are evidence of flawed thinking. It's not my job to raise children. It's my job to raise fucking adults!

It's trendy for adults to call the younger generations "weak." They're not wrong; most of the twenty- and thirty-somethings I see are pretty whiny. But they point in the wrong direction. If our children aren't the adults we want, we didn't raise them properly. It isn't the kids' faults; it's the parents'. It's the Marxist bullshit taught in schools and the materialistic garbage programmed into them because parents have lazily allowed a vacuum to exist that will be filled.

Kids crave learning, and if we don't provide it, you'll look elsewhere. I don't want you learning values from scumbags, douchebags, or other bags, so I try to teach you morality. You'll emulate my behaviour and do as I do, not as I say. Leadership's root word is *lead*. Parenting is the most basic form of leadership there is. If I want you to behave a certain way, it's up to me to model that behaviour.

I've watched parents abrogate their responsibilities to their children by over-parenting, raising perpetual infants, or under-parenting, turning kids into mini adults before their little brains can reason or regulate emotions. It's just as fucked up as previous generations being at war with their own children.

I'm trying to do what Army leadership training, parenting and child psychology books I've read, and therapy taught me. I'm trying to give you all the information I can, teaching you to make the best decisions for you. I have to factor in how much information you can process, how developed your decision-making process is, how dangerous the situation is, and a million other factors all in a micro-second. I try to give you as much freedom to make choices as I can, while guiding your decisions into the least harmful and healthiest outcomes possible. I try to be a well of support and love, no matter where my brain is taking me that day.

It's scarier than you think, kids. If I mess up, the consequences for you can be catastrophic. I have to be careful not to say you're doing something bad, because you won't hear that. You'll hear, "You're bad." I can't do as previous generations and dictate rules. If I say "thou shalt not," you'll disobey, then be scared to turn to me for help when you inevitably get into trouble rebelling. Rules don't work; agreements work. Agreements require trust. So I work hard at establishing trust, teaching emotional regulation, and gently pushing you forward while panicking the entire time because all I want to do is surround you in bubble wrap and lock you in your rooms forever.

It's hard, boys. But I'm trying. Hopefully, I'm not screwing up too badly. I love you.

77

PTSD #2

In which our hero relates his experience with PTSD to encourage others.

If you're like me and still kicking, I want to celebrate your strength and courage. It takes a fucking huge amount of both to just keep getting up and putting your pants on when you're carrying the extra weight of trauma. If you're not like me but love someone who is, I want to celebrate your strength and courage.

It's so hard to move past trauma. Our limbic system doesn't do that. It lets the rest of the brain use denial or repression or suppression or whatever. The limbic system remembers everything about survival, no matter how painful or harmful it may be to the rest of the body. The limbic system remembers everything painful and drags that shit out every time anything even slightly resembles the actual horribleness of a traumatic event.

The body gets activated to fight or run; adrenalin and the other stress hormones kick into overdrive. The brain fires up old, damaged synapses and whatever. And we go apeshit. Well, at least I did. Rage on. Impulse control gone. Aggression on full.

But I couldn't always tell why. To be frank, I very seldom knew why. I just knew I was angry and needed to react. I sometimes did shit I can't even begin to understand. Once, I pretty much gave away thousands of dollars in firearms for pennies on the dollar. I have entire months of memories locked away in my amygdala that I'll never be able to access. I can't recall most of my childhood and adolescence because I was so fucked up with anxiety and depression.

I knew I was crazy. I knew I was different. I knew I could never be fixed. I couldn't figure out why I did some shit, and I often regretted things I did. When I could experience emotions, they were overwhelming and took control of me. I never really felt calm or peace or joy. These emotions were unavailable to me. I learned there were times when certain specific responses were expected, so I'd laugh at jokes I didn't find funny or show sadness I didn't feel. I did it so people would stop looking at me like I was different.

I did it so people wouldn't know I was different.

I couldn't experience intimacy with another human. Not until Dixie and I'd been together for a couple years. And eventually, when she was dying and I was losing myself more and more to fear, I lost the ability to experience intimacy with her. I believe part of what killed her was my emotional unavailability when she most needed me to be emotionally present. I'll carry that guilt and remorse forever.

I scared a lot of people over the years with my sudden rages. It was so much worse when I drank. It cost me friends.

I still have those emotional outbursts. I still experience the fear. I still have all the same symptoms. But I can control the reactions much better. And I can feel. I can feel sadness. I can feel loneliness. I'm so grateful for that. Because I can also feel calm. I can feel peace. I can feel joy.

Hey, man, if I can get here after four decades of mental illness piled on trauma, piled on addiction, piled on grief, piled on everything else…well, you can too. Pick up a shovel and start digging that new channel. It was so totally fucking worth the pain to get here.

78

TO MY SONS #19

In which our hero reminds us to change negative for positive thought patterns.

When my father taught me to ride a horse, then a bicycle, then a motorcycle, he told me to always look up, look ahead, look where you want to go. The horse or bike will go where you look. Where your eyes go, your body wants to follow. The horse or bike will respond to your body. When I joined the Army and my instructors were teaching me drill, they (oh so very gently) insisted I look up when I march. Look forward. "Necks back in the collars, troops! Eyes up! Heads up!"

Look where you want to go, not where you've been. You've seen all that, and you aren't going that way. If you want to look back to take stock, get your bearings, so you can move forward with a better idea of where you've come, sure. Fine. Glance back, sure. Predators will buttonhook to get behind you. But you can't walk forward while looking back. Your goal is ahead of you. The end of the trail is forward. The tough spots on the trail are ahead of you. You've navigated the ones behind you. Look forward.

If you want to enjoy your life, get started. Don't waste any time. Your life is all the time you have. Your time is your life. Don't waste your life dreaming. Start working. Start achieving. Start becoming. Learn from yesterday. Apply those lessons today. Make tomorrow better. I love you.

79

BACKS AND BRAINS

In which our hero equates physical to emotional injury to reduce stigma.

Some days I can work out for twenty to thirty minutes.

Some days I can't put on my socks without help.

It's humiliating.

But that's what it is, so I gotta deal.

I buy tall boots that don't lace up for that reason.

Some days I can maintain and regulate.

Some days I have fucking tantrums like a toddler.

It's humiliating.

But that's what it is, so I gotta deal.

I take my meds and try to practise my therapy for that reason.

Like Dennette reminds me, my brain, like my back, suffered a lot of trauma, and sometimes it flares up.

It's an injury.

It's not my fault.

I don't try to make it happen or even let it happen.

But sometimes it happens.

Rehab the back, rehab the brain, and work to make them healthier to prevent the flare-ups.

If you're not doing yoga or Pilates, start one of them right now.

Seriously.

If your back isn't wrecked, these things will save you.

If your back is wrecked, these things will help you.

If your brain is wrecked, and you're not doing therapy, eating healthy, exercising, getting twenty minutes of sunlight a day, practising gratitude, and establishing emotional connection to another human being, then fucking start.

These things will save you.

If your brain isn't wrecked, these things will still help you.

80

FEAR-BASED AGGRESSION

In which our hero uses allegory to explain fear's connection to mental illness.

I had a dog named Meg. Sweet dog...gentle, kind, loving. One day, she witnessed our other dog, Lady, get attacked by a pit bull. Pit bulls aren't inherently violent, dangerous dogs. Unfortunately, there is a certain type of dog owner who is an insecure, overcompensating douchebag, and they poison all their relationships, including the one with their dog. It turns their dog into a violent, dangerous, insecure, overcompensating, douchebag dog.

After that, Meg would attack any dog her size or larger that came near. She lived "offence is the best defence." It's called fear-based aggression. Scared dogs attack. Most animals only get violent out of hunger or fear, really. Including humans. Classic example being the stereotypical bully. A bully is an insecure, violent, overcompensating douchebag. Reflection of society, really. Society is comprised of fear-mongering leaders and media, and fear-ridden public, so it uses police and corrections officers to inflict violence on its marginalized and disenfranchised members, thus perpetuating the cycle of failure.

Funny thing is, humans are operating on fear-based aggression all the fucking time. Nobody wants to acknowledge it, let alone deal with it. We'll treat our dogs for it, or put them down if they can't be treated, but we won't take care of ourselves or those we care about the same way…just a thought.

Meg responded poorly to my attempts to modify her behaviour. Yelling at her…swatting her butt…choke collars…none of these things worked at all. Weird, huh? Using force and violence on an animal traumatized by violence proved counterproductive.

So. Weird.

Then Dennette moved into the house and started treating the dogs and me with kindness. We all responded better. We all also started responding to each other better. Our relationships improved exponentially when we began to treat each other with kindness, respect, and empathy.

So. Weird.

Meg had to be put down after a year or so of Dennette living with us, but it's because of old age. She went out quiet and peaceful, with a Wendy's bacon burger on her breath. I still miss her, and I still regret how badly our relationship went for a bit, with both of us being nuts from fear-based aggression.

Every single decision we make is based on emotions. Every single decision we make is based on fear. Every sensory perception we have gets scanned through the limbic system for threats to our survival, and that lizard brain can't distinguish between physical threat and psychological threat.

Learn to understand your fear. Learn, or suffer forever from fear-based aggression, yours, or someone else's. You or someone else is or will become an insecure, overcompensating douchebag. Fear is the enemy, but like Sun Tzu said, understand your enemy and understand yourself, and you'll win every battle.

81

TO MY SONS #20

In which our hero reiterates positive behaviours to prevent mental illness.

Flowers grow from shit and mud. Your environment doesn't dictate who you have to become. Who you were isn't who you are, and who you are isn't who you have to stay.

Just because someone doesn't see it your way doesn't mean either of you is incorrect. And maybe, just maybe, neither of you has to be right. Maybe they ain't wrong or crazy. Maybe they're just dancing, and you refuse to hear the music. Listen harder.

Remember the Rules and the Principles: if it ain't right, don't do it. If it ain't true, don't say it. If you say it, do it. If you don't want to do it, don't say it. If it needs doing, do it, like it or not. When you do it, always do your best.

Help people when you can; don't harm anyone unless they force you. Own your shit. If you did it, say so. Never quit. If you started doing it, finish doing it. Every time you're scared, you've an opportunity to be brave. I love you.

82

JOHARI WINDOW #2

In which our hero details the importance of the Johari window.

Why is the Johari window important? Well, because I said so! No, seriously, because we can't see our own shit. Our shit gets in the way. Fucking deliberately. Our crazy knows if we can see it, we can get rid of it, so it hides itself. And…here's where it's so brilliant…it hides itself behind itself.

I can't always tell the difference between when I'm freaking out and when I'm legitimately upset. Dennette usually can. But she can't always tell when she's being irrationally upset and when I'm an asshole who legitimately deserves her anger. If we don't find the courage to drop our bullshit defences, other people can't learn enough about us to see who we truly are and therefore can't help us regulate when we're being fucking bananas. If we aren't strong enough to reveal ourselves to other people, devoid of insecurity-driven fear of judgment, we can't honestly see ourselves.

You can't put down something you don't know you're carrying.

You gotta accept your shit. Until you stop suppressing, repressing, denying, and running away from your shit, you can't make it go away, and it'll continue to own you. Until you face it and accept it, you can't let it go. And if it's hiding itself from you, then you can't face it and accept it. You need someone else to show it to you. Maybe that's a trusted friend; maybe it's a professional therapist; maybe it's in group therapy; maybe it's a stranger you meet on an airplane. But unless you allow others to help you push back the boundaries between the known panes and the Unknown panes, you aren't going to get to know yourself well enough to fix the shit you need to fix.

More, though, if we don't allow others to truly know us by lowering our defences, we can't become. We can't grow if our shit is in our way. We can't achieve and accomplish and flourish. We don't live, not to our fullest potential. We merely exist.

We grow and achieve and accomplish and become through necessity quite often. Necessity is the mother of invention and all that. A few become and grow because they're just wired that way: the elite athletes, the mind-bending artists, the self-made rich.

But there's usually some demon driving them, and so, many live in misery because, for all their achievements and wealth, they haven't faced that demon. So we have celebrities on the covers of magazines and splashed across the internet who're also in rehab, dying of overdoses, or just going apeshit bananas. Sadly, if these miserable "success" stories only had the courage to be vulnerable and lower their defences to a trusted someone, that person could probably help them reduce the Unknown panes, and they could fix their shit.

If we can summon the strength and find the courage to allow others in, we can explore ourselves. We can learn about ourselves. When we gather knowledge on any subject, we find ways to use it to our best advantage. Imagine how that'd work if we gathered knowledge about ourselves. If we can use someone else to learn about ourselves, devoid of the inherent biases we have and the outright lies we tell ourselves, we can discover our true potential, without having to depend on the uncertainty of fate bringing some misfortune on us to bring forward some hidden part of us.

Why is the Johari window important? Because it helps us stop being crazy. Why is the Johari window important? Because it helps us become the people we were born to be rather than the ones we settle for.

83

PUT THE DEVICE AWAY

In which our hero explains the harmful effects on the brain from electronic devices.

My family gets angry with me because I insist on trying to limit the amount of time they spend on devices. There are far more negative properties to screens than positive. They're just psychologically fucking garbage, to be frank. (The irony of writing this to you on a laptop hasn't escaped me; don't worry.)

There're so many studies proving the unhealthiness of screens that it's not even studied as "is it bad?" but "how bad is it?" The screens themselves are bad for you, especially if you stare into them at night, when getting ready for sleep. Your brain knows it's getting light through the eyes, so it isn't time for sleep. The later into the night you stare at a screen, pouring light into your eyes, the harder it gets to fall asleep. Turn off your screen an hour before bedtime. (Do I need to explain the horrific effects of sleep deprivation? There's a reason it's used in interrogations.)

That's just the screens. That's just the device itself, and it's already fucking up your emotional state. Let's explore the harmful effects of the garbage on those screens.

Social media. Lies and damn lies. Every minute on a social media platform exponentially increases your odds of depression. If you're already battling depression, fuck's sake, what're you doing on social media? How many people do you need lying to you about their lives? Do you really need to rate your life against an imaginary bar?

Kids and screens. Holy shitballs. Seriously? I need to talk about this? Studies about the negative consequences of television on children's minds go back half a goddamn century. Every hour a child spends on TV, never mind the constant barrage of instant imagery on the internet, increases the likelihood of an attention disorder by 10 percent.

The mainstream media lies. Their job isn't to inform you; it's to provide advertising space. I know this to be factual. I've been on the front pages of three different national newspapers, and not once was the story even remotely true to the events. The media are vampires who try to suck away your money, time, and happiness. Make deliberate choices about who gets your time. Does some babbling liar deserve your time more than your children, your partner, or your dirty laundry? Not really, right?

Be there for those and focus on things that matter. Don't be overwhelmed by the spoon-fed shittiness of the media by not giving them your time. It'll reduce your stress exponentially. You'll start putting your attention where you should: living beings who deserve it and your goals. How're you going to achieve what you want if you're pissing away time on things that get in the fucking way?

I haven't paid attention to the news in a decade. If it forces itself into my awareness, nothing's changed. The media uses fear to manipulate the public, who then demand their political leaders remove more rights. It's always the same, fear-mongering and doom-saying. Fuck that.

Television and movies are more vampires sucking away your life. Their job isn't entertaining you; it's selling you garbage. Sucking away your money and the time spent earning your money. You want to be entertained? Talk with someone entertaining. Television literally makes you dumber. When you read, your brain has to create images. Screens remove that necessity, so part of your brain stops functioning. And it's all the same stories, anyway. I can't watch television or movies with my wife because I always predict the ending in the first ten minutes. Stop demanding bread and circuses and go outside.

Read a fucking book. You cannot learn everything through experience. You ain't gonna live that long. There is a universe to explore, so read lots of books. If you want to improve your life, you need knowledge, and that is found in books. Somebody has devoted time to write those pages, to impart their gathered knowledge and experience for you. Somebody cares about that subject and has tried to give you a foundation to build upon.

That's what books are, you know. Another person's knowledge given to you to use. The more you read, the more knowledge others give you. Learn from them and build. If you read, you'll improve your odds of succeeding in anything. If nothing else, reading teaches you how to learn. And that is a priceless gift. We spend so much of our time in search of mindless "entertainment" that we've forgotten how to learn and can't teach our children. *Qu'est-ce que fuck?*

Go be the person you were born to be. I promise you, you weren't born to waste your time, body, and brain cells letting a screen tell you what to do and what to think. You're way better, way more than that. Do you really need to piss away your life working in a box, to live in a box, so you can stare at a box that makes you stupid?

Turn off this device. Go. Be.

84

JUDGMENT #3

In which our hero connects and explains the harm to individuals and societies from judgment and control.

I sit here reading university students rant against all the brainwashed, racist, patriarchal, misogynistic Nazis that provide their oh so very comfortable way of life (y'know...their parents?), and I cannot help but sigh. I have to read some newspapers to find specific articles, and the comments below each article are so filled with hate and vitriol and outright unscientific bollocks, it makes me fear for the species. (I'd just close the laptop and work out, but I've a paper due.) Anywho...

Whoa, now! Ease on up there, Judgie McJudgerson. Throttle back a tad. Lift your skirts, or lower your pantaloons, and untwist your knickers just a mite. Be a little less furious. Stop trying to hurry us. Be a little more curious.

You'll get a lot less triggered, and your relationships will all improve, and your life will get so much better; I can't even... ugh. Okay. Here's some advice for all y'all that'll truly help you and everyone you know and just make the world a better place. Put a helmet on; buckle up.

Here's the thing…all those people who think differently than you? The ones who stubbornly refuse to think what you tell them they have to think? They're not brainwashed. They're not stupid. They're not even necessarily wrong. Well, maybe they're brainwashed. Just as brainwashed as you are. If you automatically assume the other side is brainwashed and only your side knows the truth…congratulations, you're brainwashed. Stop drinking the Kool-Aid.

You wanna know how you know your "side" is nine kinds of fucked up and just as wrong as the other "side"? You wanna know how you know your "leadership" is as phony as a three-dollar bill and just as much a buncha lying assholes as the "other" side's leadership? Here's how: when both "sides" are saying they want to make the world a better place for everyone but don't ask anybody else what that looks like for them. When both "sides" insist on telling everyone else how to live their lives. When both "sides" are deciding for everyone else what their better world will be, regardless of anyone else's thoughts or opinions.

Pure judgment. What's judgment, after all? It's also referred to as "othering." Othering is terrible. Results in awful things, like slavery, genocide, rape, and war. Othering is the exact opposite of what we, as humans, really need.

Y'see, when you're mentally ill, the first thing your illness tries to do is isolate you. And the cure for depression, anxiety, PTSD, and addiction, is human connection. Soooo…othering is both a cause of, and a result of, mental illness. Also primitive thinking.

In most Stone to Iron Age cultures, the name each culture or society gave itself meant "the people," and the word for "enemy" and for "stranger" were the same. Ancient Latin used the word *hostis* for both, ancient Greek used *xenos* (hence *xenophobia*), ancient Hebrew used *zur*, the Ute nation gave us the word *comanche* (that nation calls itself "Nʉmʉnʉʉ"), and my Indigenous ancestors used *ayahciyiniw*. Tribalism meant survival, and xenophobia meant control over scarce resources. Conformity to expected norms was vital to demonstrate tribal fidelity. Tribal leaders (and they were usually secular and religious—separation of church and state wasn't a thing until quite recently) used this tool to keep power. And so the immense power of judgment is brought into play, along with shame, along with insecurity.

Let go of the judgment. It's just a mask for fear. It's mental illness. It's Stone Age thinking. You're better than that. We're all "the people," and a stranger doesn't have to be an enemy. You can meet them with an open hand, not a fist. When you do, most will shake yours.

All that insecurity, that fear…it's weight you don't need to carry. It's weighing you down. Let go of it. Stop those thought patterns. Replace them with healthier ones.

It's especially stupid to hear people shit talking people for wanting the exact same thing as the "other side" and being manipulated by assholes in office. Dude, that "other" person? They grew up in the same country, same culture, same society you did.

The same influences that created them and their "stupid" ideas created you and yours. They're you. You're them. Stop trying to battle insecurity by making them the bad guy. That's why you're all fucked up and stressed out, y'know. They don't have to be wrong for you to be right. You're probably both wrong, anyway. And until you accept that possibility, you can't find out who's wrong or right, or where. If you listened to each other, you'd both gain.

Just like you can't be brave until you're scared first, you can't learn something until you first admit ignorance. Maybe that other person knows something you don't. Maybe they know what you know but see it differently. Once you accept you know very little and you need other people to fill in blanks, you start to feel less insecurity and fear.

Let go of the need for control. You can't learn if you already think you know everything. You can't find real answers if you won't ask yourself questions. A closed mind is a useless mind. Sacred cows make the tastiest hamburgers.

We all think we're the leading actor in our own personal movie. Problem there is, you think I'm walking onto your set, and I think you're walking onto mine. Neither of us knows the entirety of the other's movie. We each get a snapshot, and we decide we know everything we need to about the other actor. The extra in our movie.

We're both wrong. Neither of us has access to the full script. But if we listened to each other, we'd probably figure out more of the plot. And we'd enjoy our movie a lot more. Caramel popcorn, or some shit. Besides, neither of us knows what the fuck is going on. Somebody else handed us the script.

85

OPINIONS AND ASSHOLES

In which our hero connects opinion and mental illness.

Maybe only assholes hang on to opinions. We form instant opinions and base our behaviour on them when we don't have near enough information on most subjects to have an informed opinion on anything. Somebody, maybe a friend, maybe a clown on an internet website we follow, spouts off some bullshit, and we decide to believe it because it's easier than finding out the actual facts. We get our opinions, our "script" handed to us, and we take it as gospel. It ain't. There is no gospel truth. The universe is too complicated and beautifully chaotic for any of us to grasp the truth. But if we all listen, we might learn more of it than we knew before.

Rule 4: help those you can. But don't waste a lot of time or energy on worrying about their opinion of you. In fact, don't waste any time or energy on giving a shit what they think of you. Their opinion is their problem; don't make it yours. That just makes you have to defend your opinion, and it probably isn't worth defending; you probably don't have an informed opinion. Just an opinion. I don't know about you, but just trying to figure out what the fuck is happening in my head is hard enough; I can't be bothered to give a fuck about somebody else's shit.

It's tricky; I get it. How do you achieve two seemingly opposing things at once, right? How do you maintain the human connection so vital for psychological stability while obeying the built-in, programmed need for social acceptance and not give a fuck what other people think? Try empathy. Try vulnerability. Try honesty. They're hard. They're scary. And they're the only way to get where you need to be. Be brave. Brave enough to be vulnerable. Be strong. Strong enough to be honest.

Nobody is a nobody; everybody is a somebody. When we try to dismiss another person as a nobody, when we try to negate their entire existence, that opens up a can of worms very few people have the stomach to look into. That's a scary Freudian slip that should make you rethink your shit. It's overcompensation for insecurity, and it's so big. When somebody calls anybody "a nobody," well, it's abundantly clear, deep down, the person trying to negate the other is pretty sure they, themselves, are, in fact, worthless. That's horrible and it's a super sad way to live. I know. I did for years. It sucked.

It's crap anyway. It's simply not factual. Everybody has potential. Most of us waste that potential, but it's there. That means everybody has value because everybody has the potential to do something incredible. Everybody is a somebody because everybody can do something special.

Including you, too, by the way. Everybody needs to be seen, heard, and understood. Try to see the other. Try to hear the other. Try to understand the other. Pretty soon, you realize they really aren't "other" at all. And then you stop othering. You stop judging others. Eventually, you even stop judging you. Try to be kind. It's the easiest way to influence others' opinions of you toward the favourable, and if it doesn't, it influences your own opinion of yourself for the better. And it just makes the world a better place to be in.

86

FIGHTING IS LIFE, LIFE IS BEAUTIFUL

In which our hero uses prizefighting as an allegory for the battle against mental illness.

People question me about the apparent dichotomy between my new-found pacifistic behaviours and the fact that I love watching combat sports. Between not wanting to hurt anyone ever again yet still training to be able to. Between teaching my sons non-violence yet insisting they learn martial arts.

Well, first, until we can all figure out how to stop interacting based on fear, I'll need to defend others from insecure, over-compensating men like I was. Until we realize our fear creates fear in others, y'all are gonna need people like me, who'll stand between you and people who use violence for their own ends. Sadly, I cannot see the day where people like me, who will fight and die for those who won't protect themselves (but who look down on us, pretending their fear is morality) will no longer be needed.

Second, it's neither new-found nor pacifism. The martial arts are about achieving a state where you can see other people aren't enemies. Once you've reached a level of competence that breeds confidence, it becomes about conquering your true enemy: fear.

Random quotes from *The Book of Five Rings*:

> There is nothing outside of yourself that can ever enable you to get better, stronger, richer, quicker, or smarter. Everything is within. Everything exists. Seek nothing outside of yourself...

> The ultimate aim of martial arts is not having to use them...

> Today is victory over yourself of yesterday; tomorrow is your victory over lesser men.

And from *The Art of War*:

> If you know the enemy and know yourself, you need not fear the result of a hundred battles. If you know yourself but not the enemy, for every victory gained you will also suffer a defeat. If you know neither the enemy nor yourself, you will succumb in every battle...

> The greatest victory is that which requires no battle...

> To win one hundred victories in one hundred battles is not the acme of skill. To subdue the enemy without fighting is the acme of skill.

If Miyamoto Musashi or Sun Tzu says something about martial arts, it's pretty much a lock.

Why do I love combat sports? Because they're the purest form of competition: two people of equal development and mentality. Teamwork is vital, but once in that cage, ring, or on the mat, it's just you and your opponent. Without your opponent, you can't become more than you are. They're trying to defeat you, but they're what makes you improve; your opponent is your partner. It's beautiful.

Combat sports most purely, to my mind, reflect life. Life is a fight. Everything that lives does so at the expense of other living things. Less literally, we all struggle at times. We all fight for something against something at some point. Life is about the struggle. Life is hours and hours of grinding in the gym. Life is learning, growing. We can't all be the champ. But anybody can be a contender if they work hard enough, long enough. Very few of us do. Most of us are scared to try because we might fail.

Failure isn't catastrophe. Failure sucks, but it's necessary to learn. Humans don't learn from success; we learn from failure. We learn from overcoming obstacles. If you've never failed, you've never attempted anything. And that's a sad way to live. Those people are easy to spot. They're the loudmouths spending all their time mocking others, usually through sarcasm because they think it makes them sound witty.

I don't always cheer the champ. I've rarely been the best. Okay, I've never been the best. I often cheer for the underdog. Because they dared. They did more than every asshole sitting on a couch or bar stool. They're a fucking champion, even if their hand isn't raised. Because failing is better than not trying. The loser never tries. They're losing at life.

I've lost fights, both on a mat and on concrete. I know how that sucks. Not the physical pain. Cuts heal; black eyes fade. No. The psychological pain sucks. The humiliation and failure. But if you're a fighter, you start again. You do work. You find the courage to fight again. If you've learned, then you haven't lost. You're still ahead. And the longer it takes, the harder you have to work to get there, the sweeter victory is.

I fight. Every day. All day. I fight the thoughts trying to drive me into depression. I fight the anxiety trying to debilitate me. I fight my ignorance, seeking knowledge. I fight my inherent laziness and strive. I fight to be a better dad. I fight to positively impact the people I meet in this world, because in the next, nothing will go with me but reputation.

I fight with empathy, kindness, and compassion. I fight the cold cruelty of an uncaring world, trying to bring light to the dark places in someone else's head. I fight to achieve victory over myself of yesterday. I fight to be a better man. My battles are fought inside as I strive to become the man I was born to be, as I learn about the worlds inside and around me. Fighting is life, life is beautiful.

87

TO MY SONS #21

In which our hero encourages us to overcome insecurity and self-judgment to achieve mental well-being.

My sons, despite anything and everything I can do for you, you're going to make mistakes. It's okay. It's more than okay; it's mandatory. You won't learn until you screw up.

You're going to fail at shit. It's okay. It's necessary. You won't learn how much it sucks to fail until you do. Let failure spur you to greater efforts.

Never let fear of failure stop you. Try everything. In fact, don't just try, dare! Dare greatly! When you fail, fail epically, then try again. Epic failure is the best kind. It means you've aspired. You've dared. You've lived with guts and with gusto. You've lived large.

Epic failure is something the tepid and weak will never have the privilege of experiencing. They'll quit too soon or never dare in the first place. We call the people who try heroically, whether they succeed or not, "heroes." They're inspirational, so be inspired. Then be inspiring.

Most people will never understand the glory and joy of giving everything and failing in the attempt. The wondrous learning that comes from striving and failing, then striving again. These people will mock you for failure. They do so out of fear.

They trick themselves, believing the path of least resistance they follow is the correct one. They do so because they know better but want to believe living in mediocrity is the best choice. They do so to lie to themselves in an attempt to convince themselves the illusion of safety found in the middle of a herd is the correct path. They do so to excuse their own fear.

Ignore them. The lion doesn't turn his head because a little dog barks. A champion is a contender who just refused to quit. Flowers grow from shit and mud. Diamonds are created by applying pressure. Seek pressure. Seek challenge. Seek failure; it's the opportunity to learn.

Attempt great things and you'll live a great life. Attempt great things and you'll be forced to learn, to grow, to gain knowledge and skills, to hone talents through hard work. Aim as high as you can see, and you'll be forced to work as hard as you can and become a better person than you thought possible.

Once you've done that, you've succeeded. You're living a great life, and you've achieved a great thing. You're extraordinary. Live extraordinary lives. I love you.

88

JUDGMENT #4

In which our hero correlates opinion, judgment, and insecurity to explain underlying factors of mental illness, individually and societally.

Y'know what I've learned in my fifties? I've learned shit is way more complicated than I ever thought possible and way simpler than anyone wants to admit. Stick with me; it'll make sense in a bit. First, we gotta differentiate between knowledge and opinion.

Knowledge is vital; opinion is utterly without value. My neurologist has knowledge about my back. I've an opinion. His knowledge trumps my opinion. I can't believe that even has to be explained, but it does nowadays, with everybody and their dog thinking their opinion carries the same weight as an expert's knowledge.

Almost nobody knows everything about anything. But everybody wants to pretend they do, mostly out of insecurity. So they form an instant opinion and decide opinion matters as much as factual knowledge from an expert.

Don't do that. It makes you look as stupid as you were scared you'd look if you didn't pipe up with whatever bullshit you just spouted off. Ironically, by giving up the perfect opportunity to shut up, you made yourself into the dolt you were afraid of looking like.

Wait a second. Learn some shit about stuff. In fact, learn everything you can about everything you can. And take every opportunity to keep quiet. Leaping to conclusions only results in missing your landing. It's hard; I know. Especially in this age of sound bites and talking heads and social media. Everybody is an expert when there's no consequences for them. If you think you know everything about something, you're probably wrong. Walk into every situation assuming the other person knows more than you do and you're wrong about everything. Now you're in a place where you can learn.

Ironically, the only way you can be an expert on any subject is by always assuming you don't know anything about that subject. And for fuck's sake, don't go thinking you're an expert because you're listening to the news or reading garbage on social media. Sound bites aren't knowledge. Headlines aren't knowledge. Random posts or memes from assholes who substitute sarcasm for wit aren't knowledge.

Besides, I'm going to bet you collect all your news from one source, which means you aren't getting informed; you're getting programmed. You're locking yourself into one viewpoint and fooling yourself into thinking you have knowledge. Assume your favourite news source is lying to you, and look into what their competition is saying. Both are lying to you, but you're getting a broader view of those lies.

Why the digression into knowledge versus opinion? Because judgment is opinion, and opinion is without value. Opinion doesn't allow shades of grey, but nothing is black or white. Not even polar bears. Opinion doesn't allow for the inevitable apparent contradictions where two things are true at the same time but appear paradoxical. The universe is magic, man. Shit is crazy, and we don't even have the slightest handle on any of it.

Judgment is the same thing: locking yourself into one viewpoint with no shades of grey or contradictions. Judgment prevents access to the magic of the universe. Judgment is us forming an entirely unfounded opinion on someone without knowing the entirety of their story. We assume we know everything about them that we need to. It's called "being an asshole."

Hanging on to opinion means we can't gain knowledge. We get trapped by insecurities into not allowing knowledge because it'd mean having to admit we aren't experts. It allows us to feel we have knowledge, granting us a false sense of control in a universe that is magically chaotic. Judgment does the same. It prevents us from learning about people, understanding their viewpoints, and thereby enhancing our own knowledge base.

It's ridiculous. How the fuck are you going to learn everything there is to learn about me in an instant, when I've known me for over fifty years and I'm still learning about me? Johari window. You don't know shit about me. I don't know shit about you. Judging gives you a false sense of control but prevents you from actually knowing anything about me. Judgment prevents you from learning about yourself from people you might never have met. Suspending judgment lets you see nuance and contradiction.

Eventually you don't need to control everything or overcompensate for insecurity. You recognize the only thing you can control is you, and you can rise above insecurity because you can learn something. And that becomes exciting, not scary. You can be comfortable in discomfort. You choose to release the need for control, and that is, in itself, an act of control.

No matter how much you may learn, you'll never know everything because you cannot know what it is you don't know. So you have to keep learning. You can never know everything, but you can try, and it's exhilarating. You get to learn about everything, especially you. Your relationships become more fulfilling. Your life is enhanced.

You know what I know about pretty much everything? Nothing. Just like you. I don't know everything. I don't need to know everything. But I want to. Learning everything I can makes my life better and teaches me about me.

So, yeah, shit is way more complicated and way simpler than I ever thought possible. It's complicated in that I have to keep resisting the urge to leap to conclusions to form opinions and pass judgment. It's simple in that I know nothing because the universe is way more complicated than anyone wants to admit. It's simple in that I can stop worrying and learn something every day. Until my last day. Who knows what I can learn after that?

89

JUDGMENT #5

In which our hero illustrates connection in healing mental illness.

You can't punish the mentally ill out of mental illness. You can't punish addicts out of addiction. You can't punish the poor out of poverty. Punishment doesn't work. (I thought we weren't supposed to do victim-blaming anymore. Didn't we all agree to that years ago?)

Kindness and compassion usually fix shit. Mental illness causes addiction, and vice versa; both cause poverty, which causes both. You want crime to go away? Start working on fixing one of the above.

Y'know, it's been ten months since I walked off my job in the jail. Since then, as I no longer continually judge others or judge me, my brain has healed so much…I'm so often calm. I laugh now. Really fucking laugh (without forcing it because it's the appropriate social response). Like, from the belly and spontaneously. I don't remember a time when I lived this way…content, I guess?

I used to be so crazy, hardened felons have urinated themselves, knowing I was coming for them. Trained Law Enforcement Officers have puked, knowing I was coming for them. Now I put love notes in my wife's lunch and make happy faces on my sons' pancakes. As a friend said, "The perfect example people can change. From sixty grit to ten ply."

Canada doesn't have a justice system. It does have a legal system, though. Complete with professional, actual, literal judges. Judgment is only ever harmful. And that's the problem. The system is based on an inherently flawed idea. What do you want to do about it?

90

TO MY SONS #22

In which our hero illustrates how to prevent/overcome mental illness.

Success isn't monetary wealth or fame. It is being comfortable in your own skin and living the life you want to. You won't be on your deathbed wishing you'd spent less time with people you love and working more at a job you hated.

If you want success, follow the Rules and obey the Principles. If you speak the truth and keep your word, you'll learn to be comfortable in your skin. If you work hard, you'll find a way to live life on your terms. This'll take courage, honesty, perseverance, and accountability. If you help those you can, your deathbed will be surrounded by humans who cannot bear to see you go.

The most courageous thing I can tell you is don't fear looking foolish. If you concern yourself with the opinion and judgment of other people, you'll lack the courage to take risks. You'll lack the courage to admit ignorance and thus cannot learn. It's okay to look stupid to people who don't have the courage to do the same. Why seek the admiration of people who fear to do what you have the courage to attempt? If you don't fear the judgment and opinions of others, you'll build the life you want by seeking paths they'll never walk.

Be kind. It's hard. It takes courage and strength. It'll draw the mockery of weaklings, fools, and cowards. This only proves how weak and foolish and cowardly they are. Selfishness is cowardice. That's why mental illness presents itself as self-obsession. Mental illness is fear exemplified. Fools and cowards will pass judgment because they're afraid. Piss on 'em. Be better.

Try new things. Try new foods. Try new hobbies. Try new things. You'll fail at some things, at times. Accept it. Look forward to it. It's your opportunity to learn and improve so that you may succeed when you try this new thing again.

Again, don't give a fuck what others think of you. It takes great courage to learn to ignore the opinions and judgment of others. But once you learn to do it, you can become free. You can learn because you don't fear ridicule should you fail. It's empowering and liberating. You're chock full of potential, but you won't fulfill it if you don't strive. You won't strive if you fear the judgment of others. Growth requires change, and change is frightening. Not least because the judgment of others will cause us to judge ourselves harshly. If you don't give a fuck, or half a fuck, or a tenth of a fuck what others think of you, you'll be brave enough to try, to fail, to learn, to try again, to grow, and finally, to succeed.

You'll learn to be comfortable in your own skin, and this'll give you the freedom to live the life you want to have. And that is the life I want you to have. If you can recognize self-judgment as merely the false opinions of others manifesting as judgment, you can dissect it. You can study it. You can see it's bullshit. You can see you're lying to yourself about yourself. If your own judgment on yourself is bullshit, how much more irrelevant is the judgment of people who don't even fucking know you? Your judgment of someone else is meaningless to them and to the universe. Why should their judgment of you have any meaning, then?

Go. Try. Fail. Learn. Try again. Succeed. Live the life you want to have. I love you.

91

FUCKING WRITE

In which our hero details the value of journalling to treat mental illness.

Write out your emotions and reactions to them. Write down your horrible life events.

Write down the good things in your life. Write out the things in your life you're grateful for. Write down your goals, short and long term.

Fucking write. Just write.

Not texting or putting some shit on a meme.

Fucking write. With a goddamn pen.

When you write, you're engaging more parts of your brain. You have to make your hand hold the pen, move it across the paper, and keep the sentence on a straight line.

Writing programs your brain toward accomplishing goals.

Writing mentally sets your inner calendar in motion and gets you thinking about timelines.

Writing gets your subconscious working on solutions.

Writing your traumatic events in detail serves to allow you to explore them from a different perspective.

And perspective is reality.

Writing them out can let you look at the events from a third-party viewpoint, even an unbiased one, perhaps.

Studies have proven (and I've personal experience with this, too, so I know it works) writing out your traumatic events can serve as a release valve and let out some of the emotional strain they cause us to carry.

Writing out your shit helps your entire brain work on it, process it, and even find ways to let it go and allow you to move through it and past it.

Writing it out can lessen the pain and symptoms of PTSD, and it can (ask me how I know) create post-traumatic growth.

Writing my shit out has shown me how to find and create positive change and positive choices.

Writing out the things I'm grateful for in life has also proven immensely helpful.

The brain can only focus on one thing at a time.

When I was all fucked up with depression, I could only focus on the negative aspects of life.

By writing about the things I'm grateful to have in my life, my brain became unable to think about the negative, hurtful things I'd otherwise obsess over.

Fucking write!

92

FUCK YOU, BEAR

In which our hero explains PTSD allegorically and gives advice for helping.

I've heard PTSD described as an invisible injury. I'm not sure I agree with that. Perhaps the actual wound itself isn't visible, but the effects sure as fuck are, right? Everybody can see how weird we are. How we don't fit in. How we don't react to things the way we should. How we're freaks. Yeah, it ain't invisible.

I've also heard it described as always seeing a bear nobody else can see. That description makes a lot of sense to me, and I use it all the time when talking with Dennette about some aspect of my behaviour that's causing us strife. She uses it quite regularly too. It's a good analogy. When you struggle with PTSD and/or anxiety, your mind and body behave like you're being faced with an angry bear all the fucking time.

That's a really good description, for those of you who don't deal with this shit. Imagine the reaction your body and brain would have if, right now, a big ol' brown bear waddled into the room with you and decided he was feeling snackish. Try to imagine the sheer terror. Try to feel your heart rate skyrocket. Try to hyperventilate. Try to feel the tingle in your bladder as your body tries to void itself of urine because it's focusing all of its energies on survival functions. It doesn't care if you pee yourself; it has to run away from a fucking bear. Try to make your eyes lose peripheral vision as they develop tunnel vision on that bear. Try to make your ears stop hearing most of the world as you fall into auditory exclusion. Try to make your fingers lose their ability to conduct small motor functions. Try to be terrified.

That's anxiety. That's PTSD. Our brain reacts to everything like that. A trip to the grocery store is as dangerous as facing a hungry grizzly.

So, why am I going over this ground I've already taken? Well, because it's Yule again. Which means Christmas parties. It means social gatherings with friends, co-workers, and family. It means social anxiety on an epic scale. It means fear if you're like me. It means working yourself up to be able to not work yourself up. Spending days in advance of one of these godawful, horrific shindigs to remind yourself there is no danger, and you can do this, and you can remain calm, and you can even find moments in there where you're comfortable and possibly even content, so just fucking relax for fuck's sake.

Except you're lying to yourself, and you know better than to believe you. But, like the rest of it, it does get easier. Trust me. I've got no reason to lie to you. (Hell, I probably don't even like you, so lying to you would take more energy than it's worth.) It ain't easy yet—maybe it never will be—but it's easier.

If you're not like me, well, you probably know someone who is. One in five Canadians, according to the stats. You know one of us, at least. If you're not like me, but you know someone who is, try to remind yourself they're fighting an invisible bear when they start to withdraw...when they say "no thanks" to some activity either before or during the social event...when they disappear (physically or otherwise) for a while. Maybe they need a kind word. Maybe they need you to piss off for a bit. Ask 'em, and then do that thing they need. Make their Yule a tad less hellish. A tiny bit less anxiety is the best present you could ever give someone.

93

PARENTING

In which our hero details how we can prevent mental illness from infecting the next generations.

I've been off work for like, nine or ten months now. Home all day, every day, with my kids. My wife has been home the last five or six months, recovering from surgeries. All day, every day. Just us. Just the four of us. Cooped up in the same house with each other, day after day.

It's been magical. I'm so incredibly grateful to have been given this opportunity. To really get to immerse myself in my family. To cherish them. Spending every second of the day with them, usually in the same room, has taught me how to truly find peace and joy: it's found in loving your family.

I've heard, believed, and repeated so many bullshit myths about parenting over the years. No goddamn wonder our entire society is a trainwreck, emotionally speaking. Hopefully this keeps you from making the mistakes I made. The mistakes generation before generation before generation made and taught to their kids.

I get sick of hearing guys say, "I need time away from my family because it makes me a better husband and father." I used to say shit like that. Back when I was insane. How does it even begin to make sense? That's the same thing as saying, "I need to not ride my horse because it makes me a better rider."

Or "I need time away from the rink because it makes me a better hockey player."

Or "I need time away from my video game because the less I play, the better I can play."

Here's the thing (stay with me now): the more you do anything, the better you become at it. That's why we do a thing we call "practise" when we want to get good at something. You want to be a better husband and father? Spend more time and energy being a husband and father. We don't get better at things we don't do.

Absence does *not* make the heart grow fonder. Connection makes the heart grow fonder. You want to be a better husband, spend time and energy listening to your spouse. Treat your partner like they're your best friend, and soon enough…they fucking are! Honesty, compassion, empathy, vulnerability. If you can't do that shit with your spouse, you can't do it at all, and that means you're broken. Relationships are work. So work hard.

Your kids are driving you crazy? Because they're always around? Because they talk to you? Because they want to be with you?

Dude, the more time you really spend with your kids, the more time you want to spend with them. Stop being pissed off they're interrupting your bullshit and listen to them. If your kids aren't the kids you want around, then stop failing them and be a goddamn parent. Leadership is modelling the behaviour you want your subordinates to exhibit. There is no more blatant example of leadership than parenting. Took me way too long to learn that.

I grew up around cowboy folk. Cowboys and cowgirls are pretty decent folk, overall. Most are quite intelligent and, despite the stereotype, extremely literate. Every one of them says their children are the most important thing in their life. Most have read hundreds of books and articles on horsemanship, saddlery, veterinary matters, feed, and all manner of general equine matters. Don't know a single one that's read a single book on child psychology or parenting skills. None can even see that they love their horses more than their kids. Their kids may not comprehend it, but they feel it on an emotional level. Generations, emotionally cut off from their kids, and teaching their kids to be emotionally numb.

I see it all the time. People learn everything they can about things they care about. Hardly any of my buddies have read any books on parenting or child psychology. Guess they ain't too interested in their kids. Except, they are. Of course they are. And that's why the cycle never stops. People just do what their parents did, or swear they'll never do what their parents did and then…do what their parents did.

If, instead of sending their kid to their room because the kid is having a tantrum, they just held the kid, to allow serotonin and oxytocin to do their job, and taught their kid emotional regulation, that kid would be so much better prepared for life. Instead of sending the kid into a segregation cell because the parent is afraid of their own emotions. Instead of subliminally teaching the child they're inherently bad for experiencing perfectly natural emotions like all humans do.

Parents today are doing what they were taught. Right? That's why this isn't anybody's fault today. But…if, instead of getting angry (which we know is a secondary emotion, right?) at their kids and sending them away because they're annoying, they were to invest some energy and time into their kids at that moment, they'd be a lot less annoyed with their kids.

I preach the value of connection in treating and curing all of life's ills, right? Well, I honestly can't think of a more important connection than between a dad and his kids. Unless it's between a husband and his partner. Maybe that one, right? Hard to be a good dad if you're busy being a shitty husband. Ask me how I know. I excelled at it. I was a fucking grandmaster of shitty husbanding, back when I was crazy. But I learned.

I was told in several different ways, when Dennette was pregnant the first time, there is no manual for being a parent. There actually is. There is an entire section in bookstores dedicated to parenting. I bought and read seven books. They were pretty redundant, which I found comforting. Meaning there really is a fucking manual. I was too crazy to put all of the lessons from those books into action for a while, but I got there.

You want to get good at something? Riding a motorcycle… playing a guitar…poker…crochet…baseball…jab-cross-hook

combo…anything. Learn the knowledge and practise the skills.
It's no damn different with husbanding and dadding. Learn the
knowledge and practise the skills.

You'll thank me. I promise you.

94

TO MY SONS #23

In which coffee and a clothing brand inspire advice on preventing mental illness.

So, it's 0112 hours, and I'm up for the night. Anyway, I'm leaning against the counter here, drinking coffee and looking at a Lululemon bag on the counter...lotta really good stuff printed on it, I gotta say. Let's explore, shall we?

You get the time to do the things you want to do by doing the things you need to do. You get the money to do the things you want to do by doing the things you need to do. You get the time and money by allocating your energy appropriately. It's called discipline. It'll be exerted on you, and at your expense, by things outside your control unless you control the one thing you can: you. Want more time? Stop wasting it. Want more money? Stop wasting it.

How you see the world and your place in it, your outlook on life, is a direct reflection of how much you love yourself. If you can love you one-tenth the amount I love you, you'll be alright. Because I love you endlessly.

Your successes are directly influenced by how you deal with setbacks and obstacles. How you deal with them is determined by how you see them. Perception is reality to our brains. Maybe they're neither setbacks nor obstacles. Maybe they're opportunities to learn. Change your perceptions.

You have two ears and one mouth. Never miss an opportunity to shut up. Listen twice as much as you speak. When you do speak, ask questions. Communication is difficult enough because every person's experiences are unique, and every person's understanding of a word is slightly different from everyone else's. Learn what the other person's definitions are. Your happiness depends on your relationships; relationships depend on understanding; understanding depends on communication.

Life, liberty, and the pursuit of happiness is a mistake. Life and liberty will give you happiness; pursuing happiness is the cause of unhappiness. Gratitude breeds happiness. Try a little kindness, like Glen Campbell said.

Never give more time and attention to the things that matter the least. The things that matter the most should take up most of your time and attention. People you love matter more than money. Things that matter most mustn't give way to things that matter least.

Breathe. Pay attention to your breathing. Let go of yesterday. Let tomorrow come. Be present. This enhances calm and breeds creativity. It's hard to be creative when you're anxiety-ridden, depressed, or rage-filled.

Supplements and vitamins really are a good idea; science finds new value in different minerals all the time. But don't buy into diets and food fads. Try to get the nutrients you need by eating as healthy and varied a diet as you can.

You're gonna die. Accept it. Now imagine it. What do you want to look back on with joy and pride? Go do those things. Go love those people.

Read books, lots of 'em. Travel, but to interesting places; screw tourist traps. Listen to everyone, then think about what you've heard. Dance in the grocery store. Sit in silence. Brush and floss. Sing.

Don't treat the earth like a dumpster. Don't treat your body like a dumpster. Don't treat your brain like a dumpster. These things are related.

Whatever it is you want to do, do it now. Tomorrow is an idea, not a promise. Plan. Save. Invest. That pension may not exist in twenty years.

Jealousy is literally counterproductive. So is envy. The more jealous you are of your partner, the more stupid shit you'll do to drive them away. The more energy you spend on hating someone for their achievements, the less energy you'll have to put toward your own. "I will" is productive; "I wish" is counterproductive.

Multi-tasking is bullshit. Your brain can only focus on one thing at a time. Whatever that is, do it to the best of your abilities. Your conscious mind can only hold a single thought at a time. Make it a positive one.

Average people live average lives. Average is the middle. It is as close to (or far from) the bottom as it is to the top. Mediocrity is stagnation. Stagnation is rotting. Average is existing, not living. Comfort isn't a goal; it's the opposite of having goals.

You're neither a cactus nor a camel. Drink more water. Ever see a houseplant that needs water? Ever see it after Mom or I water it? Hydrate. It's always a good idea. It heals the mind and the body. So does yoga.

Apply the scientific method to everything in your life: every thought, every belief, every opinion. Examine them all. If it can be disproven in any way, it isn't fact, merely hypothesis. When you do this, it strips away false beliefs and opinions. It removes the proclivity to judge. When we judge others, it is because we've been taught to judge by being judged. We then judge ourselves and almost always find ourselves wanting. We fear being seen as wrong because we fear the judgment of others should we be imperfect. Relish being wrong; don't fear it. Being wrong is the best way to learn something new.

When someone's actions piss you off, hold up a mirror. Do you see yourself in those actions? Perhaps, then, we should extend some grace to that asshole, either the one over there, pissing you off, or the one in the mirror. Maybe both?

(Those last two weren't on the bag, but they're good advice anyway.)

I love you.

PART TWO

THE
ROADMAP

95

THE MAP

In which our hero delivers on his promise of a roadmap back from the brink in a way that's easily digested and, hopefully, fucking funny.

I digested this shit over three to four years, and I'm smashing it down your throat in a couple hundred pages. Of course, I had to relearn everything repeatedly. That's mental illness; we have to get beaten over the head with the things we need to do. And we need to figure out how to stop doing the same thing over and over, expecting different results.

It's not easy. Depression sucks all the energy out of us. It's so fucking hard to do anything when we're depressed. But hard isn't impossible. You've been doing stuff you've had to so far; you can do this, too. It's so hard to do anything when we're fighting anxiety. The fear takes over, and everything we tried to do gets undone. Everything we want to do is almost impossible. Almost.

So I laid all this stuff out in no specific order. It isn't Step 1, Step 2, and so on. You don't have to do things as they're laid out. But you'll probably have to check all the boxes. Good news is, most of it's the same stuff, so there's a lotta overlap. Every journey begins with a single step, and the first step's the hardest one to make. With me now, right foot forward, and…step.

What's the first step on the journey back from hell? Let go. Let go of trying to control things we cannot control, like other people. Take responsibility for the things we are responsible for, and control the things we can to meet our responsibilities. You can control you, so do that. Mental health is affected by, and affects in turn, our physical health, and vice versa. So control the physical health; it's easier and provides help with the battle for mental health.

If you're using intoxicants or any other addiction as a failed coping mechanism, stop. Get the help you need, and stop. Addictions are comorbid with mental illness, and they feed off each other. Stop the addictive behaviour by whatever means work best for you. Addictive behaviour poisons our relationships, bodies, and minds. We need all of them to beat mental illness. Addictive behavior add to the shame we already carry and isn't fucking ours in the first place. Drugs and booze especially make it harder to recover from mental illness.

Get proper sleep, as much as you need for optimum health, but not more. Learn the tools to get to sleep. Talk to your doctor, and take meds if you need them to stop the endless racing thoughts that prevent sleep. Lack of sleep leads to mental illness, and mental illness prevents sleep. Break the circle however you have to, except self-medicating with substances (see above).

Exercise regularly and as strenuously as is safe for you right now. Endorphins are the body's natural antidepressant. The healthier your body is, the healthier your brain will be physically. The brain's physical health is just as important as its mental state. Mental illness is trackable by functional magnetic resonance imaging (fMRI) because it physically affects the brain. So physically improve the brain's health. If you don't know about exercise, the information is out there for free.

Proper nutrition. You are what you eat. Garbage in, garbage out. If you don't know the ins and outs of nutrition, learn. There are thousands of reputable websites, authors, and magazines devoted to physical health that you can use. Basic nutrition, no diets. Learn how to feed your body, and find ways to make yourself eat when you know you should. A rough guideline my wife and I use is to avoid the centre aisles in the grocery store. The food is found around the perimeter: the fruits and vegetables, meats and breads. If it comes in a box, bag, or can, it really isn't food; it's a product.

Here's where I get hypocritical because I drink way too much coffee, but stimulants like caffeine and sugar are not our friends, and depressants like booze are flat-out our enemy when we struggle with mental illness. Most folks, not just the mentally ill, find they feel better when they stay away from sugar, caffeine, alcohol, preservatives, and produced foods. There is no miracle diet that will cure mental illness, but eating well absolutely improves our physical and, consequently, mental health.

Make your bed, and tidy your home; environment reflects and affects mental state. Control your environment and improve your mental state. I learned this in basic training, and somebody showed me a cool video by an American Navy admiral who gives a great speech on this. Be wary of obsessive tidiness, though. That's not healthy and was one of my symptoms. I would freak out if a towel was in the wrong place. It became a failed coping mechanism. Don't do that. It makes everyone else crazy. Nobody can live up to those expectations. It's your illness driving a wedge between you and your support.

One of the tools I used was routine. As long as I had my routine, I could regulate better. When my brain wouldn't let me do things, I could always fall back on routine. It gave my life structure and the semblance of control. Of course, I took it to an extreme and made it an unhealthy coping mechanism because that's how I roll. Maybe you need a loose sort of schedule, without iron-bound times and days, like I had. Whenever my schedule was thrown off, I'd explode into uncontrollable rage. Don't do that. It's not helpful.

Go outside. Get sunlight. Our bodies crave sunlight, just as a plant does. We need that vitamin D! Up here in Canada, winter can be a real bitch to get sunlight, but try to get twenty minutes a day. Touch grass or a tree or snow or anything real. Get away from manmade concrete and asphalt just for a minute or two. Pet a critter. Connect with nature. I promise, it'll help.

Try to have fun. Man, I really struggled here. I'd start doing shit, have an anxiety attack, and create a whole new trigger. I didn't always have fun, but then I couldn't experience fun back then. Still, I made myself go into the world and do shit, no matter how much I dreaded it. Sometimes I'd feel better and find energy I didn't know I had because I was doing things I used to before my world turned into a steaming manure pile. Try to create. Writing helped me access closed off parts of my brain. If you're into music or drawing or woodwork, do that.

Pursue old hobbies or sports. Do something that used to give you pleasure, and you might start to feel that again.

If your doctor and you decide meds are part of the solution, accept that it will take a while to figure out which meds. It can be a real bitch to work through the various meds and their potential hormonal or physical side effects. And coming off some of them can be rough. Don't fuck with them. If the doc says take them for this long, don't stop because you feel better. Because you'll stop feeling better.

96

WARNING, OR CAVEAT, OR WHATEVER

In which our hero provides a heads-up about potential potholes in the road to recovery.

Don't try to make all of these changes at once; do it gradually, incrementally. I'd decide, "Fuck yeah! I'm gonna do all these things right fucking now!" But of course, it wouldn't all take with me at once, I'd forget and backslide into my normal unhealthy behaviours, and I'd beat myself up for not doing it all perfectly. Then I'd tank and have to start all over again. And that's demoralizing and exhausting. It would often drive me deeper into depression, and the cycle would start all over again.

On that note, don't try to do too much of anything at once. Break shit down into manageable chunks. Set goals you know you can achieve, not ones you think you should be able to. *Should* is an enemy. Illness will use *should* against you. Be wary of *should*. *Should* is judgment, either from others or, worse, from ourselves. I "should" be doing better. I "should" work harder. Yadda yadda yadda, blah blah blah. Fuck that.

Lists were helpful when I was ill because my memory was shot to hell from stress. But my illness would create lists that were too long, so nothing got done, and I'd melt down. That way, it could rub my nose in failure and remind me how much I suck at life and what a piece of shit I was. Maybe you can't clean the house, but have to focus on one room. Maybe you can't do the dishes right now, so you empty the dishwasher. Shit like that. Do a small task, then another. Eventually, everything gets done, and you've accomplished something.

97

THE HARD STUFF

In which our hero begins to talk about the mental steps necessary on the road back to recovery.

So that's the physical steps. That stuff we can control more easily. (That's almost sarcasm. None of that's easy. It's all simple. It's not easy.) Now the hard stuff. The mental stuff. This is the shit that I struggled with for years. Trying to reprogram my brain. Having an anxiety attack or flashback, forgetting everything I'd learned, and having to learn it all over again. Getting ambushed by the same triggers coming from unexpected angles. Getting caught by some unrecognized trigger. Finding myself outflanked again, driven back, and having to regroup to retake the same ground.

Realize right fucking now this is not going to get fixed fast. It took a long time to get here; it's gonna take a long time to get out. There are gonna be setbacks and slips and episodes and all kinds of shit. Never quit and you will triumph. Our demons can only defeat us if we quit. There ain't no unicorns and rainbows and shit here. It's a long, hard slog through the awful shit we don't want to deal with.

Slips and episodes and shit can be debilitating, especially if we feel like we've made real progress. But try to see it from a realistic perspective. (Which is really fucking hard, I know. I couldn't see anything realistically for years.) Yeah, sure, you've lost a little ground, and it may feel like you're right back where you were, but you're not. You've made progress; you've taken steps; you've gotten a little better. You've regained some control.

It may feel like you've lost ground and maybe you have, but you can get it back. You've already been here. You can reclaim that ground because you know it already, you're familiar with the terrain, and you can charge it faster, more fearlessly. Now you can gain new ground. Because you've got momentum.

Accept this is going to be the hardest fucking thing you ever do in your fucking life. Pick up your shovel and work. Only we are responsible for our recovery. It's all on us. It's unfair; I know. We didn't ask for it, we didn't want it, and now we have to do all the work to fix it. I know it's unfair. Doesn't change anything. Only you can change you, so get after it.

Believe that the destination is worth the work. Know that. Have faith in it. When everything is falling apart for the millionth time and you don't have any strength to try again, believe the destination is worth the effort and try again. It's worth it. Believe that. Believe in you. I do.

Know the science behind mental illness so you know it's treatable. Know the stats so you know you aren't alone. It's not just you. There're millions of us.

Seek out medical and mental health professionals. Can you do this alone? I dunno. Maybe. Have you so far, though? I can say that whenever I tried to fix my injury without professional help, I made shit worse. Can you do it without help? Maybe. But why wouldn't you use every tool at your disposal to heal? Would you try to cure multiple sclerosis or cancer without medical help? Would you slap a Band-Aid on a sucking chest wound and call it good?

Be honest. That's the hardest part, I think. Because to be honest, we have to stop lying to ourselves, and we've been doing that for so long, we don't even know we do it anymore. But honesty and responsibility are key. Once you reach a point in your recovery where honesty is an instinct and a habit, you start to see how lies manifest as judgment and stigma. Once you choose to live a life of honesty, you find freedom and calm. I'm very excited for you.

Be kind. Be compassionate. To you. Remember, we're responsible for taking care of everyone in our life, and that includes us. Treat you with the same compassion and care you would anyone else in your life that's hurting.

Understand mental illness is not your fault. It happened to you, like catching a cold. But nobody can cure your illness but you. Not a shrink, not a priest, not a spouse, not a parent. You. It's not anybody else's responsibility either. It's yours. Shrinks can serve as guides, as providers of advice, as givers of support, as impartial sounding boards, as dispensers of medication, but they can't "cure" your illness. It's your brain; it's your illness; it's your choice. You can do it. I know that.

Connect. I promise, those people who were in your life before all this shit happened and loved the fuck out of you are still there and still do. This was the hardest step. That's why it's the most important one. Find someone safe to speak to about your emotions and fears. They don't have to be a trained professional; it's not their job to fix you. It's their job to listen, with compassion and empathy, holding back judgment or problem-solving, and do their best to hear you. Start with one person. A friend, sibling, clergy member, teacher, or sports coach. Not a bartender; that's the wrong place.

If you're like me, and fighting complex PTSD, understand that relationships are part of our triggers. It's hard to feel safe because we've never been safe in relationships. I had to teach myself how. It was tough on both my wife and me, but we got here. If you're battling PTSD, your entire nervous system is fucked up from being in fight-or-flight mode for too long and too often. So I had to teach my body to relax. I did it by first teaching my brain to chill the fuck out. Took years to make my brain understand that it was allowed to feel all emotions and my relationship was my safety zone, not a war zone.

It's going to be hard. We're fighting our brain, and it's going to put obstacles in our path. This roadmap is all smooth and shit. The actual road is rocky as fuck and full of potholes. Ask someone who'll ceaselessly initiate contact to check on you regularly, no matter how often your brain won't let you get back to them promptly. If you can, have them drag your ass out for coffee or something. Pick them carefully, okay? If they're not empathetic and don't understand the nature of mental illness, they can be part of the problem. If the idea of talking to them doesn't make you feel safe and supported, they're not the one.

Our tribal ancestors used banishment as the ultimate punishment. Think about that. Mental illness banishes us. It drives us into our misery and pushes away everyone we care about, whispering in our ears that they're leaving us because we aren't worthy. That's how the crazy protects itself. Isolating us is how it keeps itself alive. It knows once we feel the support and love we crave so desperately, we'll get better.

The crazy fears connection because it knows it will fucking die! And it should die. It should fear you, and it should die. None of that was ours to carry, and we were not put on this world to be miserable. We were not born to be lost in pain and grief and loneliness and fear. That was not our inheritance. Get rid of it. Become the person you were meant to be before you got lost, before the weight became too much for anyone to carry alone.

We all need to feel that we are seen, heard, and understood. That has always been the cure to my shit. On my own, I couldn't create, let alone keep, a rational perspective, and trying to maintain the fight alone was too much. Also, because I couldn't tell which thoughts were rational and which weren't, I'd find myself on the wrong road. And if I listened to the wrong person, someone as ill as me, I'd get further down that road, and the walk back was so fucking hard. The demoralizing effect of coming to way too late and seeing the carnage in my wake was debilitating. I'd tank and crash for weeks.

Find the right people. People who make you feel respected, safe, and cared about. People who can listen without offering opinions or judgments, or try to fix your shit. People who're fine with letting you feel whatever you're feeling and sitting in that emotion with you. They're out there. (Mine came to me and kept me alive. I cherish them forever, although I rarely speak with them. They know who they are.)

Pets are great. They listen well, don't judge, and need us to take care of them. They give us love, support, responsibility, and purpose. They are not a replacement for a human, though. "Crazy cat lady" says "crazy" for a reason.

The person closest to you may not be the right one. If you've been struggling for a long time, you've infected anyone living with you. You've both created failed coping mechanisms that feed off each other. My anxiety triggers my wife's anxiety. My depression triggers hers. For years, we couldn't talk it out because she didn't understand what was happening to me and had no idea anything was happening to her. One more reason a professional is handy.

The problem is, mental illness, by its very nature, makes it almost impossible to ask for help. But *almost* is not *is*. It's gonna try to fuck with you. Be ready for that. It wants you isolated, to keep feeding off you, so it'll lie. "They don't care," or "you're flawed," or "hide your shame," or "you don't deserve them," or other bullshit. Even the voice saying you're too tired to reach out is a lying sumbitch. If you can tap your phone for the internet, you can text someone. Your brain's gonna say shit like "You're a burden and will drag them down," or "Asking for help is weakness." Lies. Whenever you help someone, you feel pretty good, right? Yeah, so do they. They fucking love you and want to help. They'll feel good, and they deserve that, right?

Okay, you think I'm full of shit; there's nobody in your life to help. I was there. Make new connections. This is super hard and scary, but once rolling, it's literally life-saving. Connections who validated my emotions let me feel safe trusting people, which helped me create relationships, and it became a healthy circle of healing.

Join a support group. Take a class or join a club. Combine two positive tools and take fitness classes, like yoga, or join a sport club. Exercise and social connection at the same time. Being with people who shared interests made me feel less alone. Being with others who were facing the same struggles with the same injuries and illnesses was even more empowering. I truly understood I wasn't alone, wasn't flawed. Sharing the same experiences and thoughts and feelings let me know it's the illness, not me, and I wasn't the only one.

Online is a good start, if you can't find the strength or energy to go in person, but it's not the same. Virtual is not a substitute. At some point, we hafta get face-to-face with another human and feel connection. Face-to-face with someone who can empathize is the best, and maybe only, way to truly get that validation.

Receiving help is vital. Giving help is just as, or maybe more, powerful, than receiving. Volunteer with some organization doing good. Look for ways to provide support and care for other people. Science says our moods improve more by giving support. Be the change you want to see in your head.

98

THE REALLY HARD STUFF

In which our hero explains how hard some of the steps on the road to recovery really were for him.

"Minimize your stress." If I could regulate my stress, I wouldn't be in this mess. That's anxiety: self-induced maximum stress levels at all times. But if you can, it's good advice. I couldn't start until my meds started to work, but once they did, and I could distinguish actual stressors from nonsense, life got better. Stress makes recovery take exponentially longer. Find ways to minimize stress; if it's beyond you right now, find someone you trust (unless you're wracked with paranoia, like I was) who can help you prioritize things. Reduce stress and regain a sense of control over your life.

"Identify your triggers." Everything was a fucking trigger! Except that wasn't true. Under everything was one trigger. Maybe it got pressed by a thousand things a day, but it's one trigger. Find it. It's really, really fucking hard. Mine was feeling unseen, unheard, unworthy. That created the fear that I was right and I really was that bullshit, so I'd react with rage, until rage or numbness were the only things I could feel. Figure out what lie your illness is telling that you're believing, then you can identify your triggers.

Learn and practise techniques to help you regulate. Practise them when you're regulated, though. Trying to learn anything when you're batshit in anxiety won't work. The easiest for me was diaphragmatic breathing. Learn to breathe with your diaphragm again, like an infant. It'll activate the parasympathetic nervous system and calm you down. Quick practice: put one hand on your chest, the other on your belly. Now breathe in, but don't let the hand on your chest move. Use your belly to inhale, and feel the hand on the belly go up. It takes practice. If you can, meditation, yoga, tai chi, stuff like that every day is beneficial. I couldn't, for years.

Practise gratitude. I can't stress this enough. Gratitude has long-term positive effects on mental health. I talked about the "one emotion at a time" thing already. Take a moment when you're doing something that needs doing, and you can do it, to be grateful for that. Every day, write lists of ten things you're grateful to have in your life.

To get past trauma, I had to learn to stop avoiding hurtful memories and connect them with the rest of my brain. I had to stop avoiding the traumatic shit and work on processing it into my memories. Until I did, I was emotionally trapped in that horrible pain and loneliness. Pushing through the avoidance was the only way to ditch the shame and fear that was killing my soul.

To deal with the anxiety, I had to stop being a passive-aggressive codependent asshole and learn to honestly and simply express my needs, thoughts, and feelings. After a lifetime, it was really fucking hard. I was afraid of conflict because I didn't deserve love, so I didn't speak up. I didn't deserve to have my needs met, and my feelings were irrelevant because I was irrelevant. I had to learn to be assertive, not an asshole, to build up self-esteem in my relationships. Only then could I have safety in my relationships, and only then could I create connection.

99

THE HARDEST STUFF

In which our hero relays how difficult the road really is and prepares you, dear reader, for the journey as best he can.

Change your thought processes. Change how you think. Change the thought patterns that keep dragging you down the same shitty road to hell.

My negative thought patterns were finely developed and well engraved into my brain over decades, starting from childhood. By my late thirties, they weren't negative thought patterns; they were my brain. By my mid-forties, I was suicidal. Again. I know how the front sight of my .45 feels on the roof of my mouth. It's real sharp.

My brain would make me feel helpless to change anything. It would tell lies to prove I was worthless and couldn't improve my life. I was trapped forever. Bad things happened to me and always would. Anything positive that happened was just a set-up for the other shoe to drop on my head.

That's the depressed mind. The anxious mind is very similar, but with extreme energy instead of extreme lethargy. Mental illness made everything bleak: the future, the present, the past. Everything was shit and would be until I died. No matter how unrealistic to others this was, to me, it was unassailable logic: I was cursed by a malicious universe to suffer for all eternity.

So, you gotta learn these traps and how to get out of them. My brain did shit like make everything all or nothing, black or white, no shades of grey. Either I was perfect or I was worthless. And nobody's perfect, so I was always worthless. No matter how many things might have gone right or I might have done well, my brain only saw the stuff that went wrong, to prove I was junk. Or it found ways to say that anything I did well didn't matter. How's that for a dick move? My brain insisted anything I did wrong was proof I was a piece of shit, but anything I did right didn't count.

Oh yeah, my brain had all kinds of lies it would trot out to "prove" I was worthless. One bad event meant anything pertaining to it was horrible and always would be. It would spin off from that to continue the "I'm always going to suck at everything, all the time" train of thought.

My biggest problem was my emotional ignorance. I was emotionally illiterate. So my brain would make me believe my shitty emotional state was reality. I felt like a piece of garbage, so I was a piece of garbage. I felt like others looked down on me, so others looked down on me. (Our emotions are valid, but they aren't our thoughts. Learn the difference.) I became my mistakes and misery; I felt like a failure, so I was a failure. I wore every negative feeling like a name tag, labelling myself with self-judgment.

I think maybe the most amazing thing my ill brain did was predict the future and read minds. My brain "knew" that everything I did would turn to shit and everything that would happen to me would be awful. It could predict the future. It didn't need evidence or clues; it just knew! And my brain could read minds. Since it "knew" I was a walking dumpster fire, it "knew" everyone in the world saw that. Everybody in the world knew I wasn't worth caring about. My brain knew that because it could read their thoughts.

We have to use rational thought to beat this irrational thinking. It was really hard and tricky for me because I had been so programmed for so long, I didn't know when the thought was irrational. I couldn't tell if I was experiencing depression or anxiety or something else. I couldn't always catch my negative thoughts until I was already sucked down that rabbit hole of self-loathing and misery. But I practised and learned. The meds helped, and having a shrink show me my brain's lies helped, but it took a lot of really intense work over a long time.

Eventually, I got so I could catch them sooner and faster. I also practised positive self-talk during times of relative calm and rationality. I started to be able to really challenge my negative thoughts. I told you about the first time I did that successfully. My brain was telling me I had to die because I was the worst father in the world. I was able to demand evidence, and it had none. I pointed out I wasn't the worst father in the world because the worst fathers willingly abuse their children, and

I never did. That was the turning point. After that, I was able to challenge my brain with evidence-based logic more often.

This was a real tough one for me, but when you're sure it's illness talking, don't just ignore it; do the exact opposite of what it's telling you. When it says you don't have the energy to work out, go for a walk or call a friend to do a yoga class. When it says it's too much effort to eat, grab a snack. When it says you can't manage a shower, hop in the fucking shower. When it says anything, don't just ignore it, and don't argue with it; do exactly the opposite of what it's telling you. It's your enemy, and it's lying to you.

I make it sound like I did this alone and it was easy. I didn't, and it wasn't. I had several psychologists, two psychiatrists, a cognitive behavioural therapist, and my general practitioner all helping me. And it was really, really fucking hard. The negative thoughts and self-talk were ingrained from a lifetime of practice, and they were instinctive, so I wasn't even aware they were negative thoughts. They were just thoughts.

My brain would outsmart me all the goddamn time. If it couldn't fool me with lies, it would go into a flashback or anxiety attack and undo all of the progress I'd made. And I'd have to start all over again. But it got easier once I set my mind to never quitting the fight. It got easier as I got better at seeing the false thoughts and found evidence to balance the irrational thoughts with rational ones.

Learn to recognize the lies your brain is telling you. Pessimism isn't realism. If everyone around you is saying a thought is irrational, it's probably irrational. Just because somebody yells a lie louder doesn't make it true. Learn to hear the truth through the lies your brain is yelling at you. You'll probably need help at first. How do you know your brain is lying to you when all it's done for years is lie to you?

Even when you start to challenge and disprove the bullshit your brain is saying, you might go with it anyway, out of habit. Seriously. You might find yourself knowing the thought at hand is utter bullshit and harmful, and you might go with it just because it's what you've always done. I did that a few times. Then I'd shit on myself for doing that, proving I was an idiot and a weakling. And away I'd go!

Sometimes I couldn't tell what thoughts were negative, but I could see that some thoughts were part of a pattern, and that pattern always led to negative thoughts or consequences. Then I'd work backwards from there. Or I'd come down from an anxiety attack and try to work backwards to figure out the trigger. But that brought its own distorted reasoning I'd have to sift through, like blaming someone else for my shit, or something equally stupid.

If your brain is saying shit you would never say to someone you care about, it's the illness. If there's no evidence someone else can see, it's the illness. If you can only see one scenario, but others can see several, it's the illness. Is your brain giving you advice you'd give to someone you care about? If not, it's the illness. Learn the science of the mentally ill brain, and you'll start seeing the harmful patterns your brain's created because they're the symptoms you'll find on any website pertaining to your illness.

Our goal is to find balance in the thoughts and see the difference between the thoughts and the emotions. We're trying to create a more flexible way of seeing the world and our place in it. Rigidity of thought is not healthy. When we examine our thoughts, we find the lies don't hold up under pressure. Liars, including our brains, can't keep their lies up as fast as the truth cancels them. Once we're able to challenge the lies our brain is telling us, we're well on the road back from the brink.

100

STUFF TO BE
READY FOR

In which our hero talks about the effects that a successful journey can have, good and bad, with some points about possible obstacles.

I know the book says Point A to Point B, but it ain't a straight line. This is a marathon, not a dash. Mental illness might need lifelong management, like diabetes or a permanent injury. Keep that in mind. I had to really work at being kind to myself about struggling with an illness and an injury. That was really tough for me. I had to learn (and relearn and relearn) that no two days are the same with mental illness, yet they're all the same. Several triggers, one overall trigger. Several symptoms, one disease.

When working with addicts and veterans, I learned I had to meet them where they were on their journey. I can't wish them to be further along the path to recovery. Same with me. Every day I had to meet me where I was. I couldn't wish myself better. But I could use my will to make myself do the things to get better. Eventually I got to where I believed I didn't have to stay stuck wherever I was.

Be ready for slips and bad days. Out of habit, I would try to repress or suppress emotions like sadness or anger, out of fear they would trigger me into depression or anxiety. Don't do that. It just leads to the numbing and depression. It's okay to feel sad or angry. Here's the thing: everybody has bad days. A bad day is a bad day, not the end of your recovery. It doesn't mean you failed and have to start at ground zero (but it will feel that way the first few hundred times). When you have a shitty day or a shitty event, it's okay to feel shitty about it. Let yourself sit in the sadness or anger or whatever, then, once it's run its course, let it go. It's been really helpful to me to understand emotions are supposed to come and go. Don't stay in that place. I would do that out of emotional habit, I think.

Relapses follow a pattern. Try to figure them out and look for the early warning signs. They're always the same with me, and that's been common with everyone I know. If you're not in a place where you can see them, maybe someone else can tell you shit's about to go sideways. If you can trust someone that way. I couldn't for a long time. My crazy used that to isolate me.

It's going to be really hard to distinguish between the illness and you. I can usually distinguish between someone else's illness and their actual personality. I couldn't with myself.

I had to learn (and relearn and relearn) that today's suckiness doesn't mean tomorrow will suck too. Whatever I'm feeling today, right now, is not necessarily what I will be feeling tomorrow, or in an hour. Just because I'm dragging ass today, with nothing to look forward to but another day of pain, doesn't mean I'm going to be depressed tomorrow. Just because I didn't get anything done beyond keeping the children alive doesn't mean I won't do things tomorrow.

I had to learn (over and over) that a couple bad things about an event are not the entire event. One mistake or accident doesn't ruin the entire whatever-I'm-trying-to-do. I learned, over time and with great effort, to see the positive of situations as well as the negative. But I had to continually remind myself until it got easier with practice.

Once you hit a certain stage in your recovery, expect to feel a shift in your understanding of the world. It's called post-[insert name here] growth. You might begin to see patterns of overlapping layers of nonsense and how much of our culture perpetuates mental illness. We, as individuals, can't reach true mental health if we're surrounded by madness. It creates a petri dish for fear to grow in.

You may feel compelled to try to change it, like I do, or to just walk away from it all and breathe free. Go with it. Fucking do you and roll with it, whatever it is that makes you a better you. The better you are, the better everyone around you will be. Compassion and kindness are as contagious as fear and anger; they're just quieter.

Recovery is weird. I find myself having to learn how to do things differently, which is weird because I think differently, and that's weirder. Weirdest of all, I have to learn who I am now. I have to learn how to be a different person. I have to learn who that person is. He doesn't do things the way I used to. He doesn't react to things the way I used to. So far, I kinda like hanging out with him. He's way more fun than the other guy. My wife and kids like him, too, so that's cool.

PART THREE

POINT B: BACK

EPILOGUE, OR CONCLUSION, OR SOMETHING

So there it is, folks. Everything I know about why I got all fucked up. If it rings bells, then maybe it'll help you figure out why you're all fucked up. Maybe some of it'll help us figure out why we're all, collectively, all fucked up.

If you're looking to blame somebody, by getting angry or taking shit out on yourself, you missed the whole fucking point of the book. Go back. Start over. Read it again. Blame is judgment. Judgment drives division and isolation.

Empathy, connection, compassion…that shit cures everything. Be compassionate to yourself. Connect with others. Put down the ugly shit you don't need to carry anymore.

Vulnerability is terrifying and hard and so very goddamn necessary. It takes courage and strength. Be brave. Be strong.

It's impossible to be angry or depressed when you're grateful. Forgiveness is a lot lighter than anger. Share your pain and decrease it. Share your joy and increase someone else's.

Speak the truth. Keep your word. Work hard. Help those you can. Make someone else's life less hellish, and yours becomes less like hell. Courage. Honesty. Responsibility. Perseverance.

All this shit sucks at first. Nothing worth doing is easy. Everything important in life is simple, not easy. So embrace the suck. And, hey…try to have a little fun now and then.

Love hard. It's gonna hurt sometimes. It's totally worth it.

POSTSCRIPT: SUCCESS

Well, Sheridan, it's 0412 hours on a November Monday, and that thing you're feeling? That absence of anger? That's calm. Enjoy it; you've earned it. Good for you, old man; you did it.

The older you get, the less noise you make, the deeper you think, and the wiser you become. Wisdom comes from humility, and life will humble the shit out of you. All the rage of your youth is utterly wasted on life. Besides, pretty much everything you raged about in your youth was judgmental nonsense springing from insecurity, and you wasted your time and effort.

When I learn something about myself that makes my life better, I'll keep trying to teach it to everyone else. They won't listen, but I've done my due diligence and met Rule 4. On that note, it ain't my job to save the world. I can't tell people what to do, let alone what to think. I can, however, put the best information I have in front of them so they can come to their own conclusions. Besides, I might be wrong. I know exactly jack shit about fuck all, after all. Besides, nobody asked, you arrogant asshole.

Jesus was right: love thy neighbour.

Chinooks are fucking awesome. But then, so are blizzards. The mountains have taken my soul, but I sometimes miss the desert. The world is beautiful, even when she's being a bitch.

You can't save the world. It's okay to walk back through the muskeg to help someone lost in it, but you can't walk their path for them, and they don't have to walk yours. You can warn them about the dangers, but they don't have to listen, and it ain't your fault if they don't. Walk your path; it's tricky enough. Watch your own goddamn footing.

Don't waste your time worrying about other people's opinions. Don't waste time paying attention to your own opinions. Opinions are judgment, not fact. Judgment will prevent learning. Judgment is a trap. Judgment is a prison that locks down your thinking. Judgment creates fear of judgment. It prevents creativity because it prevents the courage to experiment and explore. It prevents growth.

Albert Einstein was right: if you can't explain it simply, you don't understand it. It's always easier to get people to believe a lie than to believe they've believed a lie. If they refuse to listen, you've done what you can. If they can't understand, you're not explaining it well enough. Keep trying to find simple but intelligent ways to explain the shit you've learned about life, or you don't really know what the fuck you're babbling about.

Today, I'll become a little better than yesterday. Tomorrow, I'll become a little better than today. Keep working. Rule 3. Be smart about it. Learn to improve your ability to improve.

Shakespeare was right: we know not what we may be. Some achieve greatness. Our doubts are traitors and make us lose the good we might win by fearing to attempt. No legacy is so rich as honesty.

You're getting soft. If you want to live long enough to meet your goals of raising these kids to be adults and living the life you want to have, get back to work controlling what you can: you. Get your diet back on track. Get your workouts back on track. Get twenty minutes of sunlight a day. Get your sleep back under control. You have nobody to impress, but you do have goals to reach. Get to work.

Marcus Aurelius was right: live in truth and justice, tolerating those who are neither true nor just.

You're married to a pretty amazing woman. Make sure she knows you know that. Your kids are pretty fucking amazing too. Make sure they always know that.

The world is a beautiful place. Life is a gift.

ACKNOWLEDGMENTS

Thanks to K. Douglas, Lianne Picard, Andrew Donald, Josh Taylor, Janet Trace, Torie Carlson, Michael Hryciuk, Brian and Sabrina Dunsby, Chelsea and Dustin Munford, Leon Underwood, Mathieu Plamondon, John Zelenka, Cheryl Dillon, Jeff Schellenberg, Shelly Sonnichsen, Gary Thivierge, Lise Stevens, Terri Gillis, Bryan Chown, Sara Savard, and those of you who choose to remain anonymous, for helping fund this thing.

Thanks to Drs. Lutz, Primmer, Carlson, and Rahmani, the Veterans Transition Network, and Wayfound Mental Health Group for helping me put my brain together. (Yeah, I had entire teams working on my shit. And you think you're crazy?)

Thanks to Tammy for the TKO.

Thanks to Yannick and Erin for being my safety net.

Thanks to Jeff for the love and laughs.

Thanks to Waylon, Willie, AC/DC, and the Rolling Stones for always being there when shit got real bad.

Made in the USA
Coppell, TX
07 December 2023

25576830R00246